Entering the Mysteries

Entering the Mysteries

The Secret Traditions of Indigenous Europe

Arthur Versluis

"This is an inspiring book, in which decades of scholarship are distilled into a personal testimony. Part travelogue, part Platonic meditation, it explains how the ancient Mysteries opened up conscious commerce with the gods, or, esoterically, with one's own divinity. In his pilgrimage to the ruined sanctuary of Samothrace, Arthur Versluis discovers that its stones still carry a spiritual and even physical charge that can set the initiatic process in motion. The Greek island then stands for all the other sacred sites, in Europe and beyond, that lie ready to support a new marriage of heaven and earth within the individual."

—Joscelyn Godwin, Colgate University, author of *The Golden Thread*, *Harmonies of Heaven and Earth*, and many other books

"Dr. Arthur Versluis, one of the world's foremost esoteric scholars, takes us on a journey to the fabled Aegean isle of Samothrace, a center of the ancient Mysteries. This book is a travelogue, and not just in a physical sense—Dr. Versluis guides us on a journey through realms of myth and history to uncover the secrets of ancient Western spirituality. At journey's end, the author steers us home to who we really, deeply are."

—Leonard George, Capilano University, author of *Crimes of Perception* and *Alternative Realities*

"Lucid, beautifully written, yet based upon a vast reservoir of evidence, previously either impenetrable or largely ignored, Arthur Versluis takes us on a voyage to the hidden mysteries of Samothrace, and brings us back home to see with new eyes the continuities—and ruptures—between archaic Indo-European traditions and our own times. This book shows us how to read and experience the overlaid but still living resonances among myths, tales, philosophical texts, telestic practices and places (ranging from Orpheus, and earlier, to late Platonic theurgy) that linked and continue to link the human and the divine."

—Kevin Corrigan
Samuel Candler Dobbs Professor of Interdisciplinary Humanities
Emory University, author of *Gnosticism, Platonism, and the Late Ancient World, Reading Ancient Texts,* and many other books

"A timely and important book. The author has ventured into an almost abandoned corner of European hiero-history, a time when the gods of Greece still informed the collective life of a people long used to their vivifying presence. Reading *Entering the Mysteries* is to enter the mystery itself."

— James Cowan, author of *Desert Father, Messengers of the Gods,* and many other books

"This richly inspiring book won me over even with its sub-title "The Secret Traditions of Indigenous Europe". The starting point of the journey is the Greek island of Samothrace, one of the most potent sacred sites of the ancient world. Versluis goes on to explore the ancient gods ("all manifestations of the divine") and some of the profound symbols and mythical motifs with which the world of the ancient Mysteries was filled: serpents, centaurs, twin figures like Castor and Polydeuces, the celestial mountain, the north as the land of eternal light, and the notion of the hieros gamos or sacred marriage. Altogether a most light-filled book, which gives me hope that the secret traditions of indigenous Europe have a future as well as a past."

—Christopher McIntosh, author of *Gardens of the Gods*, *Master of the Starlit Grove*, *The Return of the Tetrad*, and other books

Library of Congress Cataloging-in-Publication Data

Names: Versluis, Arthur, 1959- author.
Title: Entering the mysteries : the secret traditions of indigenous
Europe /
   Arthur Versluis.
Description: Minneapolis, MN : New Cultures Press, 2016. | Includes
   bibliographical references.
Identifiers: LCCN 2016012140 | ISBN 9781596500228
Subjects: LCSH: Mysteries, Religious--Europe. | Europe--Religion.
Classification: LCC BL610 .V47 2016 | DDC 292--dc23
LC record available at https://lccn.loc.gov/2016012140

Text set in Georgia

The paper used in this publication meets the minimum requirements of ANSI/NISO Z39.48-1992 (R 1997) (Permanence of Paper).

Cover image courtesy of the author.

Designed by Katie Grimes

New Cultures Press
Minneapolis, Minnesota

Visit us at
www.newcultures.org

Printed and bound in the United States of America

19 18 17 16   1 2 3 4 5 6 7 8 9 10

Contents

Introduction

As one approaches by ship, the island seems to rise up from the sea as if out of primordial antiquity, first a long dark and misty shape on the horizon, with its own bank of clouds, then its mountainous slopes taking shape as one comes nearer, the sunlight glittering on the waves, dolphins in the ship's wake. So it is today, just as it was three and four millennia or more ago. There is something about a mountain whose pinnacle is shrouded in mist: one can readily believe that a god or gods might belong to such a place. Mount Olympus is like that, and so is Parnassus near Delphi, home of the Muses. One feels that the place itself is shrouded in mystery, and that by approaching it, we are entering into our own primordial past. And we are.

In all of antiquity, there is one place more than any other that was famous for its Mystery tradition bound up with the land itself. Kings and queens, emperors, dignitaries, soldiers, sailors, yeoman farmers and slaves, men and women, heroes and gods, all came here from the whole region, making the journey across land and across water to this sacred place whose landscape was home to gods more ancient than Greek civilization itself. Samothrace, home of the Sanctuary of the Great Gods—the *megaloi theoi*.

We were standing on the ship's starboard topside, the wind tousling our hair as we approached this most mysterious of islands. On the island's prow, we could see perched above a rock outcropping a stone tower where once the island's population kept watch for pirates or invading Turks, not necessarily mutually exclusive categories. Arriving from the sea like so many pilgrims before us, we watched as the island's harbor grew nearer, alive with bright colors under the splendid sun of the Aegean.

Our arrival was not so different from that of prospective initiates from ancient Greece or Rome of several millennia past. Like theirs, our journey had been long and difficult, fraught with obstacles and trials. It was often said in antiquity of Samothrace that if a traveler was not meant to be on the island, some turn of events in the journey there would prevent arrival. Tacitus, the ancient Roman historian, wrote in his *Annals* that Germanicus sought to travel to Samothrace to be initiated, as had so many before him, but a strong north wind arose and prevented him from arriving on the island.[1] Samothrace was known in antiquity for protecting travelers, especially those at sea, but by the same token, was known for preventing the arrival of those who should not arrive on its shores. As our ship came into the harbor, we smiled.

But where was it we had arrived? It was the same place that the ancient hero Jason and his crew of Argonauts were said to arrive several millennia before to be initiated. Among Jason's crew were the sons of gods—several sons of Poseidon, god of the sea; Orpheus, son of Apollo—and the great hero Hercules. Jason and his crew of heroes, guided by the oracle of Apollo at Delphi, sailed on a magnificent ship, the *Argo,* made from wood from Mount Pelion (the ancient home of the centaurs in Greece, including Chiron, the centaur tutor of many heroes and gods, including Hercules and Jason) and from a sacred oak of Dodona, the sacred grove west from Athens dedicated to Zeus. The oak beam from Dodona was said to talk and to guide them on their journey. And on this great ship, seeking to retrieve a magical golden fleece from the land of Colchis, they collectively went to one place to be initiated—here, on Samothrace.

Indeed, the name Jason is sometimes spelled Iason or Iasion, and derives from Aetion, a spelling in turn corresponding to that of some of the oldest names for the gods of the great sanctuary on the island. What is more, it is said in antiquity that Jason—Aetion—was responsible for the island being open to the initiation of strangers, that is, open to all who arrive and are worthy, of whatever social class from slaves to royalty.[2] In fact, Jason or Aetion was said by at least one source to have been the child of Zeus and Elektra, and the ancient name of the island was said by some to be Electris. Elektris's original inhabitants, said Diodorus Siculus, did not arrive there from elsewhere but sprang up autochthonously from the island itself.

And now we were here, on the shores of the very island that in great antiquity was called Samos, before that was called Elektris—whence we get our modern word electric—and whose gods had many names, among the oldest Axieros, Axiokersa, Axiokersos. It is possible that these three are the original names for gods of the island, and some think that they are a triad, two male deities (Axieros and Axiokersos) with one female, Axiokersa. But the whole island is itself sacred ground. It is not that the sanctuary alone is sacred, or that it is dedicated only to particular deities. That, we came to realize, is not quite how the ancient mysteries of the gods were, here least of all.

What then were the ancient mysteries of the gods? How were they conveyed? This is what we had come to this ancient and enigmatic island to discover for ourselves. We had been to many sacred places across Western Europe, in France and in England, in North America. And we had come to Samothrace on intuition, with the sense that here—whatever was here—were clues about the nature of the gods themselves and about the ancient Mystery tradition whose primordial origins would seem lost to us today. There was, we suspected, something here that would let us understand the mysteries of the ancients and the knowledge that they held.

And there was. This is, of course, our journey.

We are offering to you what we discovered because part of our purpose is to point toward the ancient indigenous spiritual traditions of Europe itself. We are offering here clues and indications, and an account of our journey, because we have come to understand how vital it is that modern Europeans and those of European descent begin to recall their ancient origins and purpose once again, begin to recognize what extraordinary riches are ours. But we must be worthy of them, or they will not disclose themselves.

This is the only book of its kind. In it, we bring you, as much as we can, into the living Mysteries of great antiquity. Those Mysteries are not lost, but present. Their presence, however, requires us to approach them in ways that we in the modern world are not accustomed to, indeed, seem singularly ill-suited to. We live in a world in which our attention is drawn outward by myriad devices and technologies, in which discursive rationality and materialistic assumptions and explanations predominate, and in which poetry, allusion, and intuition are not highly valued or often even acknowledged as having any value.

Thus, for us to enter into the world of the ancient Mysteries, we have to set aside our preconceptions and become open once again to the hidden dimensions of nature and spirit, and of ourselves most of all. The keys to those ancient Mysteries are to be found in many sources—in the clues left in the works of the ancient historians of Greece and Rome, in the myths of the gods, in the ancient stones and ruins, of course, but most of all, in the places themselves. There is a reason why Samothrace was known for its Mysteries from time immemorial. It is an extraordinary place, a mountainous island rising up out of the Aegean, ringed above with mist and clouds, inaccessible, wild, and alive.

Our ship behind us docked in the harbor, ahead of us the narrow road along the coast, we stood in the warm island's sunshine and looked, as countless pilgrims before us had, along the coast and toward the mountain and the Sanctuary of the Great Gods. We were encountering Samothrace itself, and our quest was just beginning. We had set foot on sacred ground.

Chapter 1
Samothraki

The island of Samothrace today, as always, belongs ultimately to itself alone. It was known throughout history as a somewhat forbidding destination because it did not have any good natural harbor, and though one larger and one smaller harbor has been built in modern times, the shores are largely stony and were inhospitable for beaching ships in antiquity, as they are today. Varro wrote that in Roman times there were two twin brass statues in the harbor, both ithyphallic male images he identified with Castor and Pollux, the twin sons of Zeus known as the Dioscuri in Roman mythology, sometimes said to have been born from an egg, and known as the patrons of travelers, especially sailors.[3] Similar twin statues were also said to be at the Sanctuary of the Great Gods, in the valley nestled at the western base of Mount Saos. Today, there are no such statues in the harbor, but for us, at least, they were there in spirit. They definitely represented the enigmas of this unusual place.

We traveled east along the narrow road of the island that skirts its shore, the edge occasionally eroded so much that the pavement jutted out alone over the seashore, crumbling. At times the road sank down where a drainpipe under it had collapsed, and more than once we sped up to make it across, thinking it might collapse beneath us and if we had built up a head of steam, at least we would make it to the other side. At one point, we were shunted off onto a rough dirt and stone detour because the main road had collapsed entirely. But we eventually found our cottage along the shore, only several miles from Paleopolis, the ancient city, and the nearby Sanctuary itself.

The island, in antiquity forested with oaks, today has many different microclimates. Every turn, ascent, or descent features a different landscape and vista. There are dense forests, rocky escarpments, thorny underbrush, high peaks; there are rolling pastoral lands, mountain villages, shrubby dense underbrush; there are thermal springs, high vistas overlooking the sea, where streams begin above; and everywhere, it seems, there are goats, high above, perched impossibly on rocks, silhouetted against the sky, down along the road, grazing on flowers until they are shooed away. It is a rugged, wild island still, featuring secrets hidden within secrets in its remoteness.

Samothrace takes one part of its current name from the northern region of Thrace, home of the god Orpheus, and it possesses still the wildness associated with its namesake and the god himself. Orpheus, you might recall, like all of these mythical figures, is more than a bit difficult to grab hold of, and as soon as one thinks one grasps what he means, something else comes to light that calls into question one's earlier view. That said, the myth of Orpheus reveals some aspects of ancient indigenous religion in the wider region, and in Samothrace itself. For as we come to understand more deeply later in our journey, myths express truths that cannot be conveyed literally, only alluded to. So it is with Orpheus.

For Orpheus was a poet, a singer, and a magus; by his incantations, he was able to charm wild animals, trees, plants, all of nature. Taught by Apollo himself, Orpheus played his lyre and sang. He was said to have gone on the *Argo* with Jason and his crew in search of the golden fleece, and saved them from the lure of the sirens through his songs. In time, he charmed the nymph Eurydice, with whom he fell in love. Bitten by a snake, however, she died, and he was so disconsolate that he went into the underworld to retrieve her. He brought her nearly to the light of day, but despite being forbidden to do so by the king of the dead, Orpheus looked back at his beloved, and with that glance, lost her to the underworld forever. Thus Orphic mythology is intimately bound up with charms, magic, wildness, ecstasy, music, dance, sexuality, and license, as well as death and retrieval from the underworld, and more broadly, with death and rebirth.

There are some clues about the metaphysics and meanings of the Orphic myths. On an Orphic gold lamellae (gold sheets on which texts were inscribed) uncovered in nearby Thessaly was written the following: "Who are you? Where are you from?" To this is appended the famous answer: "I am a child of Earth and of starry Heaven, but my race is of Heaven." This theme, of twin realms, and of our higher origin, is one to which we will return again in a later chapter. And Plato gives us another clue when he writes in the *Republic* that Orpheus is a "child of the Moon," suggesting he is a guiding figure for those initiators (like Orpheus's initiate Musaios, to whom the first of the Orphic hymns is addressed) into those rites that are purported to redeem us from the consequences of our ethical failures or transgressions in the past.[4] The ultimate purpose of Orphic rites is that our afterlife is a good one.

Samothrace is itself home to a mountain whose highest peak is Fengari, "the one who gleams," that being a modern word for the moon, whose earlier name was Selene. *Samos* is said to mean "great height," and thus the name of the island could be understood as the heights of Thrace. And we found ourselves on the island at night under a waxing moon nearing full, my companion and I.

I should say at this point something about my travel companion and myself. I will call her Chandhi, her name associated with Chandra, the lunar deity in Vedas associated with the mysterious elixir *soma* (it "shines") that bestows immortality. She has pale lunar skin and thick black hair like the mane of a horse; I have blue eyes and blond hair like the golden

light of the sun. "Chandhi" is, of course, the name
of the consort of Shiva the destroyer. Chandhi and
I traveled to Samothrace across much of Greece,
beginning at Athens and the Acropolis, taking the
path of the Eleusinian mysteries, then making our
way past Mount Olympus and Mount Pelion, past
Thessaloniki's great port, and on along the coast to
Alexandroupoli, whence we then sailed to the island.
We had encountered a few obstacles along the way,
gotten lost once or twice, but we had made our way
to the island nonetheless, to our bed and breakfast
surrounded by richly flowering hydrangea bushes
along the rocky coast.

We are both entirely from European bloodlines,
mine a combination of Dutch, German, Belgian and
English, and she is of Anglo-European heritage too,
so Greek in appearance as to be often mistaken for
a native. And we share esoteric spirituality as well—
Chandhi has experience in an esoteric tradition
that draws on the Mysteries, while I have decades
of experience in esoteric Buddhist traditions, and
familiarity with the esoteric traditions of the West.
We set out on a journey to this ancient mystery center
because we intuitively trusted one another, and the
place.

So this sojourn on Samothrace was, for us, an
exploration of the island and of the greatest remaining
sanctuary of the Mysteries in antiquity, but it also was
our time together to come to understand one another
more deeply, to explore the island, and also our own
relationship. The morning of our first full day on

the island found us at once at the gate to the ancient Sanctuary. At the entrance to the sanctuary, as at so many points on the island, there was a reminder of Greek Orthodoxy, in this case a small chapel that one passes as one goes over the bridge above the stream, and up the hill toward the Sanctuary of the Great Gods itself.

The Sanctuary is the heart of the island and cannot be seen from offshore, hidden as it is behind a canopy of trees. As we walked up the path toward it, hand in hand, we crossed over the stream again and then passed through the gateway into the ancient ruins, long pillars and sacred stones laying akimbo on both sides of the path, everywhere, more and more stones. The Sanctuary was thoroughly destroyed, pillaged by millennia of visitors, ruined successively by Christians and then Muslims who detested and feared the beautiful buildings and sculptures of the ancient indigenous culture here, reportedly damaged too by an earthquake that perhaps also marked the catastrophic end of the ancient Mysteries here, not to mention a succession of pirate bands right up to that of the French looter Charles Champoiseau, who managed to make off with the magnificent Greek statue the Winged Victory of Samothrace, in the late nineteenth century installed at a stairway in the Louvre in Paris. All the extraordinary buildings and images that once stood in this mysterious place are gone, and only stone outlines in the earth remain.

But what stones! And what a place! For despite the passage of thousands of years, despite the looting and deliberate destruction, despite everything, the Sanctuary has the unmistakable ambience of a place reverberant with sacred authority. We recognized it immediately. Yet what we recognized intuitively and absolutely cannot be articulated easily, perhaps not at all. We were silent as we explored, making our way past the remnants embedded in the earth of what once was clearly an extraordinary complex of buildings made of sacred stone, here the dining hall, here the theater whose seat-steps were sunk into the hillside, here the Hieron where the main initiations took place—it was like meeting an old friend, with whom one has to spend time catching up. We bathed in the presence of the place.

The Sanctuary is ensconced in a valley, really a kind of gully, behind it the height of the great peak, Fengari, while the Sanctuary complex itself is pointed out north toward the pure blue waters of the Aegean. It is hidden even as one walks up to it, hills surrounding it, and then suddenly it appears, and there, one feels the primordiality of the place, because this is where the earth rises up out of the sea into the blue sky, where the valley opens out toward the sea ahead, the mountain behind, the sky above. We are, here, even today, the first, the primordial couple.

The island has a remarkable presence, and the longer we stayed there, the more we came to recognize it. "It isn't just the Sanctuary," Chandhi told me one afternoon as we made our way from the far side back to where we were staying. "The whole island is sacred." It is indeed for us a magical place, yet it is hard to articulate exactly why this is so, and perhaps it is not so for everyone—who can say? But for us, the varied faces of the island landscape, bucolic and wild, seaside and mountainous, with steep waterfalls into placid forest-surrounded pools, thermal springs, hidden restaurants in the hills, and ever-present semi-wild goats, all remain in one's memories and dreams like glimpses from an island out of time.

It is true that thousands of years have passed since the Mysteries were celebrated here on Samothraki. Those of us from the European world no longer are aware of our own heritage, so much so that even the words "indigenous Europe" seem unfamiliar to most of us. But there is such a thing as indigenous Europe. What is more, what we will explore together in this book are enduring dimensions of human life to which we have access today just as an initiate did several thousand years ago. The sacred stones, the landscape is still there; and what is more, so too is nature, wildness, the sun and the moon, poetry, song, music, the harmony of the cosmos itself; the waves of the great sea, the mountain and the flowing waters; the forests and the waterfalls; the mysteries of humans and nature; the mysteries of man and woman; and the mysteries of humans and gods. Of all these, we will speak, as we begin to enter the mysteries not only of antiquity but, indeed, of life itself.

What are the mysteries? Who or what are the gods? What is the meaning of this profound and ancient place? Join us as we explore together what it means to be human—the mysteries of death and rebirth, of life and of transcendence.

Chapter 2
The Mystery of the Mysteries

Perhaps the greatest mystery of all antiquity concerns the religious tradition known as the Mysteries. There are a few books devoted to the Mysteries, and we do have some indications concerning them from the historical records, particularly the accounts or allusions found among the ancient historians, and from the inscriptions on stones or tablets, as well as other aspects of the archeological record. We even have a wonderful Roman novel, *The Golden Ass* by Apuleius, which gives us an account of the main character's initiation into the cult of Isis. But all of these remain, in the end, tantalizing clues for solving the enigma of the ancient Mysteries. For the initiates were famously sworn to silence, and that is a silence perhaps even more powerful today than it was millennia ago. In the end, we will enter into this silence and what it means.

Of course, we have to understand that the word "Mysteries" is applied to a whole array of quite disparate religious phenomena in late antiquity: there were Mysteries of Mother Goddesses, Mysteries of Egyptian origin, like those of Isis and Osiris, Orphic Mysteries, Mysteries of Dionysus, Mysteries of Mithras, not to mention the Mysteries of the Kabeiroi, and the Athenian Mysteries associated with Eleusis, and, of course, the Mysteries of Samothrace, only to mention the most famous. There were Mystery sanctuaries scattered across the ancient world, but particularly in the region in and around Greece.

Initiation into a particular Mystery tradition typically took place at night, and secrecy was enjoined, particularly about the nature of the initiation itself. What is so remarkable about the ancient Mystery traditions of antiquity is that thousands upon thousands were initiated—we have an extensive list of initiates from Samothrace alone, because many initiates left on the island stones or tablets on which their names were inscribed—and yet we have only occasional clues about what they might have experienced there, because no one divulged the secrets of the Mysteries. We have no detailed accounts, no metaphysics of the Mysteries, no full insider's narrative that gives us a clear indication of what the Mysteries were really about, only fragments, hints, indications. Without doubt, the Mysteries remain the great riddle of the ancient Western world.

While we today use the term "Mysteries," from the term *mystes,* meaning "initiate," the ancient Greeks used other terms, including *teletai* (from *telos,* that which concerns the end, or that which lies beyond death) and *orgia,* meaning celebration, the origin of the modern word "orgy." The building where initiation took place was often termed the *telesterion,* and at Samothrace is given the name *Hieron* (from *hieros,* meaning "sacred," or "sanctified," though we know that only because a nameplate with that inscription was found near the building we today call the Hieron. All of these terms, taken together, give us some indications of the nature of the Mysteries and, in particular, the Mysteries at Samothrace.

As the two of us stood atop the stone wall at the back end of the Hieron at Samothrace, looking out across the ruins of that building toward the Aegean Sea in the distance, we were struck by how grand the place must have been during its zenith in antiquity, when it enjoyed the patronage of the Macedonian king, when the magnificent buildings and statuary adorned this ancient place. And what also struck us was its intimacy. The Hieron, indeed, the entire ritual complex here at Samothrace must have been extraordinarily beautiful, but it was all relatively close and was not meant for crowds, or even for large groups. There were initiators here; there were kitchens and dining halls; there was a modest theater embedded in the hillside; but all of it made for an atmosphere of both grandeur and intimacy. This is where people and the gods mingled.

Earlier, I had been to the excavated ruins in Athens where lies exposed the ritual path to Eleusis (about a dozen miles away from central Athens). But the Eleusis path, unearthed by archeologists, ends just past the mound gravesite of the most ancient Athenians; it dead-ends into the wall of the modern, decaying, noisy Athenian cityscape, and one senses nothing of what must at one time have been there. It was as if an electrical line had been cut, and now while the stones are excavated and exposed, so from the far end behind one can see the sacred high points of the city to each side, to the right the magnificent citadel of the Acropolis, to the left the Lycabettos Hill, one has the sense that in antiquity the lines were alive with invisible power, whereas today they are not. One *sees* the sacred geography of Athens and how the path to Eleusis aligned with it, but one doesn't feel it.

Samothrace is different: we could tell that immediately. Outwardly, of course, the great complex there was in ruins, only outlines of buildings' foundations visible embedded in the earth, save for the five standing pillars at the northern end of the Hieron that had been erected perhaps a century before. Yet for all the ruins, the place was still primordial, the landscape and hills around, the sanctuary itself somehow partly outside of time. It was alive, alive in a way that very few ancient sacred places still are.

As we stood in the Hieron, we could sense the presence not so much of a particular god as of divinity—this is a *temenos,* a sacred place, sacred for millennia upon millennia, for time immemorial. And yet to whom was it sanctified? For its name is Ιερό των Μεγάλων Θεών (*Ieró ton Megalón Theón*)—the

Sanctuary of the Great Gods. But which "great gods" were those? Some say the Cabeiri, or Kabeiroi; others give ancient names that begin with the letter "A," like "Axieros"; some say that the temple complex at Samothrace belonged to an ancient Great Mother goddess; others say that it was associated with Hephaestus, god of metallurgy; and still others say that the Sanctuary was devoted to Persephone, or perhaps to Demeter, or again to Twin gods; or again to the sacred marriage of Cadmus and Harmonia. But what one feels when one is there is not particular deities so much as divine presence.

And this is one of the secrets of the ancient gods. As the insightful Roberto Calasso observes, in Greek the word *theós*, or "god," "has no vocative case," but rather predicates, for it designates "something that happens." Thus, "recognizing the beloved is god." *Theós* is an event, and when an event is recognized as *theós*, it is only one more step to say that it belongs to Zeus, "the most vast and all-inclusive of gods, the god who is the background noise of the divine."[5] What we experienced was the sacred as sacred *presence*—the place itself, this ancient primordial sanctuary of the unknown gods, the god of the unknown, is the sacred revealing itself as this place.

The difficulty of direct communication with the gods, the fluid or mercurial nature of the gods, knowing them through symbols or images, analogies and indications, poems, songs, and fragments—the whole ancient world bespeaks in many respects the unknowability of the ancient gods. Hence one has the widespread practices of divination—looking at physical objects for the traces of the gods, going to virgin oracles to hear the channeled gnomic utterances of the gods. The gods speak at one remove, indirectly. When one visits the sacred grove at Dodona, it is true it is dedicated to Zeus, but before it was dedicated to Gaia or Rhea—one god blends with another, female into male, Zeus and Hera. The identity of the gods is never solid. Hence is it really so surprising that the Sanctuary at Samothrace is dedicated to the unknown gods? For all of them are unknown, indeed, in a profound sense, unknowable.

And thus the Mysteries, where humans met the divine, were also unknowable. The Mysteries were a venue, a means whereby humans can be initiated into a double life; into this fleeting horizontally temporal human life can be introduced the lightning bolt of the vertical divine, the flash in the darkness of illumination. Roberto Calasso felicitously puts it this way: "Every sudden heightening of intensity brought you into a god's sphere of influence. And, within that sphere," one is suddenly on "a second stage alive with presences."[6] Thus to enter the second sphere of the gods is to be in a parallel world, where one is at once in two worlds, this one of time and suffering, but also at once in another parallel world, a twin world, if you will, that belongs to the gods.

This doubled nature is an essential clue to the Mysteries at Samothrace. For among the epigraphy found on the island and in Roman accounts, one finds only the references to the "sacred light of the two Kabiri," the "twin lights of the Kabiri," or to the "doubly sacred light of Kabiros in Samothrace."[7] This phrasing, linking sacred light and the twins, or doubled-ness, is confirmed by the memento of initiation that we know was found on the island as well, the seal of iron rings, of which at least 32 have been found (though it is rare for the actual seal to be intact). Here is my own rendition of the seal on the ring of initiates of Samothrace:

Figure 2-1. An artist's rendering of the seal of a Samothracian magnetic ring.

What do we notice about this ring's seal? First, on both sides are renderings of the twin lights, one on each side, in its own sphere. Then, in the center, in a stylized "S" shape, are twin serpents, entwined together head to tail. The image reminds one perhaps a bit of the caduceus (the staff with twin entwined perpendicular serpents) of Hermes. But the seal of the ring is distinctive to Samothrace, and it directly confirms our theme of doubled-ness, with its twin lights and its twin serpents.

And there is one more clue about these rings that we must note: they were magnetic rings, hence echoing the orientation of the Sanctuary itself toward the north. The magnetic rings thus represent a miniature version of the island and its Mysteries, not only with the themes of doubled-ness but also with the theme of magnetic north, the lodestone, and the orientation of those who journeyed across the Aegean Sea. For we will recall that Samothrace is said to protect those who travel, especially those who travel by sea, and we will recall too that it was from the peak on Samothrace that the god Poseidon was said to have watched the Trojan War, thus associating the island with that ancient god. The iron rings worn by initiates remind us of the ancient Mysteries of the north.

And as it turns out, the Mysteries of the north have to do also with the mystery of doubled-ness, of the celestial and earthly twins. We will recall that in the northern hemisphere of the night sky is found not only the pole star but also the constellation of the twins, Gemini. The Twins, in the second quadrant of the north, were associated in ancient Mesopotamian astrology with the Lord of the Underworld and rebirth, and in Greek and Roman astrology with the Dioscuri, the twin sons of Zeus, Castor and Polydeuces, who were among the band of heroes on the Argo. They were known as the rescuers of sailors endangered by Poseidon, god of the sea, who in fact was said to have given them twin white horses to ride. And, of course, Poseidon himself, in the most ancient mythology, was associated with horses—hence in some sense the Dioscuri were salvific figures not despite but because of their relationship with Poseidon. It might be noted that according to Ptolemy, the Twin stars were associated not with Castor and Polydeuces but with Apollo and Heracles, who also were sons of Zeus (the meaning of the name "Dioscuri").

But there are still more associations with doubledness in the northern night sky, for there are actually multiple ways that twin serpents are visible there. First, there is the constellation Serpens, in Greek Ophis (Οφις), which has two parts, the head (Serpens caput) in the west and the tail (Serpens cauda) in the east, with the body (Ophiucus, or the "serpent-bearer") in between in the north. The holder of the serpent is sometimes said to be Asclepius, the healer, who was able to restore the dead to life or to restore life through healing, symbolized by the way a serpent can shed its skin and be renewed. And second, there is Draco, the dragon or serpent, perpetually visible in the northern night sky, around 3000 B.C.E. the constellation that was home to the pole star of that era.

The iron ring insignia of Samothrace evokes all of these symbols from the night sky at once, certainly both those of the twins (the twin stars) and of the twin serpents, as well as the symbolism of the north. But what do those symbols mean? Henry Corbin wrote at length about the symbolism of the north and of the twins in his works on Persian mysticism, which he was well aware reflected a much older Indo-European tradition. The term "twin" can be understood not only in a horizontal way, in terms of earthly siblings, but also vertically, that is, for instance, the individual incarnated soul below and the transcendent partner, guide, or protector above. Or, even beyond that, one's twin may be understood as one's own transcendent nature revealed to oneself as light. This was the case in Zoroastrian, Mandean and Manichean traditions, wherein the purified soul can enter the world of light and be reunited with the eternal partner or twin: "I go towards my likeness / and my likeness goes toward me / embraces me and holds me close / as if I had come out of prison."[8]

In Platonic tradition, we find a long history of the celestial guide or twin, the *daimon paredros* described by Plotinus in his *Enneads* chapter "On Our Allotted Guardian Spirit" (III.4), where he writes at length about how if a soul is weighed down by bad conscience, then after death he faces his own distorted and negative self in judgement against him, whereas he who lives an illuminated and purified life is guided by and in essence becomes that which he is guided by during life. Plotinus is not alone in such concepts, of course; we find them long before, in Plato's *Phaedo,* in the tenth chapter of his *Republic,* and in *Timaeus.*[9] But it is perhaps noteworthy when Plotinus remarks that some souls may ascend to the stars and thus have star-gods for their guardian spirits; we can ascend to the star whose power works in us, and if we return to this world, we are then like someone voyaging upon a ship. But the star can remain our reference point as we voyage; indeed, the star, in this tradition, *is* our destination.

And there is still more. For it is indisputable that the Sanctuary at Samothrace points directly north, and that in the far North in Greek tradition is Hyperborea (Υπερβόρεια), the land of the eternal sun, where the people live to the age of a thousand and in which there is no war or suffering, only happiness. In this land there are many forests and there is a river, the Eridanos. It was said that Apollo (god of the sun) spent the winter in Hyperborea, and that the Hyperboreans were associated with the sacred places of Dodona (the sanctuary of Zeus), the island Delos, and Delphi. The Greeks credited a mythical figure from Hyperborea, Abaris, as a healer from the North, a variation on the theme of Asclepius and the North. The Hyperboreans correspond in many respects to a tradition found among a number of peoples, and extant in Tibet, of "hidden lands," for instance, Shambhala, inaccessible to the unvirtuous, ruled by a wise king and elders, where the people live happy lives and easily pass into transcendence. The Hyperboreans can be understood as a secret or hidden realm where the Golden Age is accessible to those who are worthy, even in a much more fallen era.

And there is still one more dimension of Samothrace that we must allude to here: the celestial mountain. In this context, the celestial mountain is a conceptual representation of metaphysical reality: one ascends toward its peak, which is in fact the peak of the far North, that is, of the pole, which is also symbolized magnetic north that guides the sailor or voyager home. The North in this context is the land of eternal light not because it is in the Arctic region (an amusing example of contemporary literalism) but rather because it is the abode of light, beyond the cycles of light and darkness or of duality.[10] The celestial mountain is symbolized, on Samothrace, by the mountain that rises up next to the Sanctuary.

We can draw an array of inferences from all of these symbolic dimensions represented in the Sanctuary at Samothrace. Above all, we can see why Samothrace was renowned across the ancient Greco-Roman world. It has so many sacred characteristics that one can think of no other place with quite so many, particularly in such a compact space. It is, after all, only a relatively small island. But nonetheless, those who came upon it in prehistoric antiquity certainly must have recognized its unique combination of the symbolisms of the island, of the north, of magnetism, of the sacred mountain, and of sacred stones. The place itself is undoubtedly indivisible from the Mysteries that were celebrated there.

Or we could put it another way. The Mysteries

could be understood as the individual's introduction into what the symbolic aspects of the island and its sanctuary represent, that is, as a portal into an expanded and deepened understanding of the human relationships to the natural and to the spiritual realms. The culture transmitted at Samothrace conveyed to initiates in essential, symbolic form a nexus of meanings and connections that put one in touch with the chthonic and autochthonic nature of the sacred stones, and landscape, and with the sea and sky, not as objects, but as sacred geography. In this mysterious place is revealed a hidden, primordial, transcendent geography. And henceforward, the individual does not exist in isolation from that second world, which illuminates this physical world with higher luminosity and meaning. North is not merely a physical but also a spiritual direction; the mountain is not just a feature of the earthly terrain but a cloud-shrouded home of the gods.

We moderns typically think uncomprehendingly of the ancient gods and myths in literalistic terms, and as a result they seem cartoonish and opaque; our two-dimensional approach is simplistic and gauche, whereas the ancient myths are in fact multiplex, integral, and subtle. The ancient myths and the gods who inhabit them are fluid and metamorphic; each provides a different but linked aspect of a greater reality. One myth leads into another, just as one set of symbolism—doubled-ness, or north, or light, or the sacred mountain—naturally implicates all the others, which need to be taken into account in order to understand the whole and the greater reality.

This multivalence is one of the reasons that the ancient mysteries remain largely inscrutable to us. As we walked among the ancient stones and on this ancient sacred ground, we recalled the myths through which the hidden truths of this place and of the cosmos were conveyed, and realized more fully how difficult it was to convey what we understood. There is a very real sense in which, beyond what I have alluded to in this chapter, there is a self-secret dimension to the ancient mysteries. They were not revealed because they *can't* be revealed in the way you might think they could be.

But there is more. We live in an era of social, cultural, political, and economic confusion and disarray, in which it seems that humans exist on their own in a world of objects and resources for exploitation. And for the most part, we don't understand the concept of a sacred place, or sacred geography; and we don't understand any longer how to understand myths or sacred stories whose heart is allusive and alluring. As a result, we do not have our own Mysteries, and we do not know how to navigate our spiritual journey in the way that the ancients did.

Samothrace gives us indications of how to navigate; it points us toward the transcendent in the immanent. It is not that Samothrace is the only sacred place—I am not saying that. One does not have to go there; there are sacred places in North America, in Great Britain, in Western Europe, in Mongolia, in the high mountains of Tibet, Nepal, and Bhutan, only to mention those that come to mind, some of which I have traveled to. But all the same, Samothrace has its own remarkable qualities; this remarkable island mountain rising up out of the Aegean is indivisible from the archaic Mysteries celebrated there for millennia.

The Mysteries, celebrated at night, introduced the initiate to the Twins, that is, to the twin lights of the mystery of the divine companion or daimon; they oriented one toward the spiritual north, and to the twin serpents, the ouroboros of the cosmos; they gave one the means to navigate the spiritual journey of this life. Above all, they introduced us to the invisible, to the presence of the most ancient gods, those that, although they have been given a plethora of names, in the end are nameless because they are presence manifested in this particular place and time, radiating from the very stones and earth. And it is to this ancient reality that we now turn.

Chapter 3
The Ancient Gods

It was said that the Mysteries at Samothrace were celebrated in an ancient, foreign tongue, even into the time of the Romans in late antiquity. The gods did have ancient names: Axieros, Axiokersa, Axiokersos, as we have seen, and those names came from a much more ancient Indo-European tradition transmitted through the eastern Phrygian culture via Thrace to the north. The Phrygian religion featured a mother goddess of the mountains and earth, known as Cybele among the Greeks, featured sitting on a throne between lions; and Sabazios, a sky god often on horseback, whom the Greeks associated with Zeus. But what relation did these ancient gods have with Samothrace? To understand the Mysteries at Samothrace more deeply, we have to understand something more of the ancient gods.

The Mysteries at Samothrace were transmitted via the Pelasgians, who preceded the Greeks, but who were they? Their name is from the Greek word *pélas,* meaning "neighbor," itself an enigmatic term for the ancestors of the Greeks.[11] The Greeks came to self-awareness by contrast with the Pelasgians. The Pelasgians, who were said to be the most ancient indigenous inhabitants of Greece, probably originally came from the east, that is, from Western Asia, bringing with them Indo-European language and traditions. Herodotus said that the Pelasgians were a highly religious people who offered many sacrifices to the gods, but did not distinguish them by name, which corresponds to the tradition of unnamed (and many-named) gods at Samothrace.[12]

But to more fully understand the Mysteries and in particular the ancient gods on Samothrace, one has to widen one's historical and contextual lens to include archaic Indo-European religion. We have already seen some of the symbolic associations with the Sanctuary and its orientation to the north, but now we need to turn our attention to the gods and their particular associations. In the Orphic Hymns, there is a song dedicated to the "Kouretes," which refers to the "bronze-beating Kouretes," warriors of Ares, "who dwell in the sacred land of Samothrace" and who save mortals who roam the sea." These Kouretes or Korybantes "were first to develop sacred rites for mortals." What's more, while they can be destroyers, they also are "mighty lords, masters of Samothrace, veritable Dioskouroi," "celestial twins," those who bring good weather, seasons, and fruits" with their breath.[13]

It is worth noting that all of these names (as well as Kabeiroi), including what were reputedly the most ancient names, the ones beginning with *ax-* or *ak-*, feature the "k" sound. *Ak-*, a proto-Indo-European root, means "sharpness," or "pointedness," that is, it is associated with weapons, stakes, nails. Likewise, the word "akḗ" (ἀκή) in ancient Greek means "point," though it also has the associations "silence" and "healing." The Kouretes are associated with weapons and the arts of war, and were also said to be those who tended the infant Zeus, hence the name "Zeus Kouros," implying that Zeus himself is in some sense a Kourete. Strabo expressed well the difficulty in separating out the mythology here: he recorded that many then claimed "the gods worshipped in Samothrace, the Korybantes, the Kouretes, and the Idean Daktyls are the same as the Kabeiroi, but they are unable to explain who the Kabeiroi are."[14]

In an epitaph for a Samothracian initiate, Isidoros Nikostratou of Athens, we read that he was "an initiate, greathearted," who "saw the doubly sacred light of Kabiros in Samothrace." And the final line of the epitaph addresses "gloomy Hades," requesting that the Lord of Death "lead this man to the region of the reverent and place him there."[15] This is important not only because it demonstrates that light played a central role in the Samothracian mysteries, but also because its conclusion calls for an illumined after-death state in "the region of the reverent."[16] In other words, we see here confirmation of what Plutarch also said about the Mysteries, that in the Mysteries "one encounters an otherworldly light, and pure regions and meadows welcome one with voices, dances, and majestic sacred sounds and holy sights, in which now the completely initiated one, becoming free, enjoys the rite, is crowned, and communes with pure and holy men."[17] This "region of the reverent" (*choros eusebeon*). The term *eusebeon* has the root eu-, the same root as "euphoric," that is, meaning happy or blissful, and hence initiates at Samothrace were termed *mystai eusebeis*. There were two stages of initiation, *mystai*, the first, and then *epoptai*, those who became "seers," or "those who have seen."

We might allude here also to Plato, who in Phaedrus refers to the ascent of the initiates who "recall the things of the other world" and who, "with the rest of the happy band," saw "beauty shining in bright light," initiates into the most blessed mystery of the gods in which "we beheld shining in pure light, pure ourselves," for there is beauty herself shining through the "celestial forms." Plato continues that he who is newly initiated "rises up out of this world to the sight of true beauty in the other." Beauty can be seen in this world, of course, but there one is initiated into beauty as it is in itself, which is accompanied by a kind of flight, as if one were to grow wings, and this is the flight of both love and madness, the flight of eros, for eros, initiation, the gods, and the other world are all mingled with the mysteries of eros and of falling in love. What do these all have in common? Ecstasy, of course.

The tradition of the Korybantes or Kourantes is that of warriors who are carried away into ecstasy by drumming, theater, and dance akin to warfare—and we should observe that they follow the great goddess, just as the maenad women following in the train of Bacchus or Dionysos were famous for their ecstatic dance, no doubt accompanied by drumming and flute. The point here is that in these archaic celebratory rites, the men were carried away by ecstasy with a female aspect of the divine, just as the women were carried away by ecstasy with a male aspect of the divine.

We could see, as we walked among the ancient stones of the great Sanctuary, that there was indeed a choral hall, as well as a Dionysian theater—in other words, that the temple complex indeed could host just such celebrations. And we knew that in antiquity there were said to be two ithyphallic statues in the complex as well, said to be in the entrance to the Anaktoron.[18] We could well imagine how the combination of a summer celebration at night (often in June, just when we were there too, under a full moon), drumming, and music, perhaps libations, and the power of the place itself under the canopy of constellations, all conduced to produce at least the possibility of an ecstatic experience for a small group with the guidance of initiated elders.

And the erect penis, as we have seen, is inextricably part of the iconography of Samothrace. We know that the Mysteries elsewhere reputedly entailed maidens carrying in a liknon or basket a representation of a phallus, and indeed, there are countless and inventive representations of erect penises in antiquity, much more than can be fully delved into here. But what is the meaning of symbols that in the modern world would seem to be among the most banned of images? We should recall that the gods Dionysus, Bacchus, and Orpheus, but especially Dionysus, represent the lifting of bans or interdicts, license, and the emergence of primordial freedom.

There have been ithyphallic figurines found throughout Europe, carved from various substances, or painted on cave walls, traceable back into prehistory for tens of thousands of years. There also are countless phallic carvings and stones, and here one has to also mention the megaliths or vertical standing stones found in profusion in sacred sites across Europe and the British isles, but particularly in certain areas on the Western shore of the ocean, notably in Brittany and Cornwall. I have visited hundreds, probably thousands of such stones. It is not often remarked, but those standing stones can be understood as a lithic represenation of korybantic rites, that is, of phalli or a band of ithyphallic men.

There were priapic statues of Hermes, known as herms, in ancient Greece, sometimes marking borders or serving as protectors of fields, crops, and regions. There were phallic representations of Dionysus at temples in antiquity, in some cases a huge phallus upon a pedestal, as at Delos, the pedestal decorated with the image of a phallus-bird with wings. Or again from prehistoric Great Britain, a standing stone phallus on one side of which is carved an ascending serpent, at the top of which is a human face.

We know that such representations are not only ancient but in fact primeval, so archaic as to belong to the farthest reaches of archaeological evidence. And we know also that representations of the erect penis are widely associated with apotropaic power, that is, with the capacity to avert disaster. We might recall that the Sanctuary was long associated with the protection of travelers, especially at sea. In the region around the Mediterranean and elsewhere, an image of an erect penis is said to protect against the evil eye; and in fact in contemporary Bhutan, many houses have a huge phallus painted on them in order to bring blessings and avert dangers.

In various books, Alain Daniélou wrote at length about the fundamental links, noted already in antiquity, between the traditions of Shiva in India and those of Dionysus in Greece. He argued that both traditions are extremely ancient, and both reflect an archaic Indo-European tradition in which the erect penis or lingam and the yoni, or representation of the vulva, underlie and infuse Indo-European indigenous religion as far back as the archaeological record takes us. He demonstrates that there are many scriptures in India documenting the spiritual significances of the lingam and the yoni.

But our emphasis here is primarily on what the images represent, because the gods are essentially particular manifestations of transcendent qualities, and images like a phallus are manifestations of transcendent principles. The phallus image invokes the transcendent principle of creative life energy, of the power of manifestation, of vitality. By its very nature, it banishes weakness, parasitism, the "evil eye"; it is pure masculinity. And as a stone pillar, it is also a stake or a nail that binds heaven and earth.

Hence for the Great Sanctuary to be marked by ithyphallic figures is to invoke the most ancient and archetypal principles of pure virility and male energy, exactly what also the Korybantes represented with their warriors in service to the great goddess of the mountains. The erection exists in relation to the feminine principle, and ultimately invokes the relationship between heaven and earth. We recall again the saying from the Orphic Hymns that "I am a child of earth and of starry heaven, but my race is of heaven." This invokes the heart of the symbolism here.

The old gods are known through symbols, especially animals, because qualities are often best conveyed theriomorphically. The ancient goddess of the mountains who had many names (Rhea, Kybele, Agdistis) was often accompanied by or incorporated the symbolism of the lion. She was often seated on a throne, and the lion, long associated with regal power, is actually one of the few animals that can generate genuine fear and awe in the human; the lion is a predator that can overpower and devour a man, even a warrior. She was known as mother of the gods, in particular, of Sabazius, and as the one who taught Dionysos the mysteries.

The ancient Greeks recognized the old gods in their mythology of the battle between the Titans, or more archaic gods, and the more recent Olympian gods. What this mythological war preserves is the truly archaic gods and a sense that the newer gods exist in continuity with the much older ones. In fact, Zeus took as consorts some of the ancient goddesses. And the great gods at Samothrace were in fact also given, in some accounts, equivalence to Greek or Roman gods. Thus, for instance, Pausanius says that "Demeter came to know Prometheus, one of the Kabeiroi, and Etnaeus his son, and entrusted something to their keeping. What was entrusted to them, and what happened to it, seemed to me a sin to put into writing, but at any rate the rites are a gift of Demeter to the Kabeiroi."[19] Here the "Kabeiroi" seems to be equivalent to the Titans (of whom Prometheus was one).

In the Hermetic and Platonic tradition, Prometheus is another name for the inner man of light, Phos (which means "light"), as opposed to Epimetheus (the outer man) who is caught by fate and trapped in the material world. Our purpose in both the Hermetic and the Platonic tradition is to ascend to the higher dimensions of consciousness beyond fate, "without the use of any other aid, save the observation of the appropriate moment" (καιρός kairos).[20] This ascent culminates in the realization of the anthropos, that is, the man of light who as above fate and beyond entrapment in the material world and its attachments and aversions. This man of light is what the Orphic

Hymns refer to in the lines "I am a child of earth and of starry heaven, but my race is of heaven." The "race," here, is the race of light. Hence we find twins: earthly man below, and the man of light above.

We have seen how bewildering the number and names of the gods are; their stories and myths seem innumerable and to us moderns, also impenetrable. And we see this in Samothrace, where the Great Gods might have Roman, Greek, Pelasgian, or some other names and associations. But we also see preserved at Samothrace the ancient language that at the time of the ancient Greek and Roman historians already was incomprehensible. And what is more, we see preserved there the namelessness of the ancient gods, the megaloi theoi, or "great gods" being their ultimate and only appellation.

The great gods and goddesses are protean. The divine can manifest itself in myriad forms and ways, in myriad aspects of the earth's landscape, the sea, the shore, the valley, the mountain, and the sky, and in myriad gods and goddesses. What we can easily miss—because of the rich panoply of the gods and goddesses and their innumerable myths—is that they are all manifestations of the divine. When humans reach toward the sacred, and the sacred reaches toward humans, the terrain where they meet is the imagination or the imaginal, that is, the realm of images and forms and archetypes visible not to the physical eye but to the inner eye. On the "far side" of these archetypal images, infusing them, is the divine.

Those of us who were raised in a monotheistic context, but beyond that, all who are affected by what we may call the monotheistic overlay on the most ancient forms of religion, often do not recognize the extent to which it distorts our understanding of archaic religion. The sacred in archaic religion manifests itself in nature, in other human beings who may in fact be divine beings, in a world that is far more transparent to the divine than is the monotheistic, let alone the desacralized modern perspectives that are its inheritors. Monotheism, seen in this context, is the assertion of exclusive hegemony for a particular tribal deity that in fact serves to block or render opaque the sacred as it manifests in nature.[21]

By contrast, the protean fluidity of archaic religion revealed the sacrality of life in all its manifestations. From monotheistic perspectives, the male and female genitals are shameful, but from much more archaic religious traditions, they in fact symbolize, reveal, and embody the sacred. Indeed, they are preeminently sacred because they are the origin of procreation and generators of bliss that transcends procreation. Archaic religion is in fact much closer to what we today would think of as magic or shamanism; it was the result of individuals learning sacred practices and lore and then putting it to work either as priests at a sacred site, for instance, Samothrace, or as independent initiators and magi working in the culture.

Diodorus Siculus, the Greek historian of the first century B.C.E., wrote about the ancient gods called the daktyls of Mount Ide (Ida) of Krete. They were, he said, called daktyls because there were ten, one for each finger on the hands. And Diodorus goes on:

> But some historians, and Ephoros is one of them, record that the Daktyloi Idaioi were in fact born on the Mt. Ide which is in Phrygia and passed over to Europe together with Mygdon; and since they were wizards (*gonta*), they practiced charms and initiatory rites and mysteries, and in the course of a sojourn in Samothrake they amazed the natives of that island not a little by their skill in such matters. And it was at this time, we are further told, that Orpheus, who was endowed with an exceptional gift of poesy and song, also became a pupil of theirs, and he was subsequently the first to introduce initiatory rites and Mysteries to the Greeks. However this may be, the Daktyloi Idaioi of Krete, so tradition tells us, discovered both the use of fire and what the metals copper and iron are, as well as the means of working them, this being done in the territory of the city of Aptera at Berekynthos [in Eastern Mysia], as it is called; and since they were looked upon as the originators of great blessings for the race of men, they were accorded immortal honors.[22]

Hence the genealogy here is from very ancient independent shamans or wizards who taught Orpheus, who in turn established the Mysteries among the Greeks.

Plato also, in *The Republic*, has Adeimantus refer to the "host of books written by Musaeus and Orpheus, who were children of the Moon and the Muses," according to which these independent shamanic practitioners perform rituals that seek to expiate sins and that "redeem us from the pains of hell." Indeed,

"if we neglect them, no one knows what awaits us."
Further, "there are mysteries and atoning deities,
and these have great power. This is what mighty
cities declare; and the children of the gods, who were
their poets and prophets, bear a like testimony."[23] In
both Diodorus's chronicle and in Plato's allusions,
Orphism reflects very archaic religious tradition.

We came to realize, as our sojourn on Samothrace
continued, that the ancient Mysteries and the rites
associated with them (*teletai*) can be best understood
in relation to Tantrism in Hinduism and Buddhism.
Tantrism, like the Orphic and other archaic religious
traditions of Europe, drew upon primal, archaic
symbolism in order to provide rites as means of
realizing our own higher dimensions and nature and
of achieving the transcendence that brings us beyond
fate, fatedness, and earthly suffering. Tantrism draws
on all elements of human life, including those labeled
by the discursive mind as good or bad, in order to
create a higher synthesis, using everything to point
toward its own transcendence.

And Tantrism both in Indian and in Tibetan variants
relies for transmission upon individual initiators,
practitioners whose practical work is that of magician,
healer, sorceror, an expert in things invisible to the
naked eye to whom some may go for spiritual and
pragmatic assistance. Such independent operators,
whatever they are termed in popular parlance, are
very much akin to what Plato and others referred
to in the pre-Greek and Greek context of individual

initiators into Orphic or other traditions.

There is an interesting, little-known source for understanding what the ultimate goal of the Samothracian Mysteries was, buried away in the anti- Gnostic polemics of Hippolytus's *Refutation of All Heresies*. In it, Hippolytus quotes a contemporary Gnostic who writes about the

> two statues of naked men in the Anaktoron of the Samothracians, with both hands stretched up toward heaven and the pudenda turned up, just like the statue of Hermes at Kyllene. The aforesaid statues are images of the primal man and of the regenerated, spiritual man who is in every respect consubstantial with that man.[24]

Here again we encounter the theme of the celestial Twin, that of the primordial man whose purity is restored through the ancient Mysteries, the spiritual man who has realized identity with the primordial man prior to and beyond the present fallen era.

Is it possible for us to fully understand what these images, those of the twin lights, the twin serpents, and the twin ithyphallic statues symbolize, after the passage of millennia? Perhaps the overlay of disapproval and shame (the very word "pudenda" means "shame") from monotheism is too great; perhaps we cannot truly grasp what the ancients meant with such symbols, let alone realize for ourselves the nature of the ancient gods.

And yet. I will leave you with a dream that I had before we left for Samothrace. I dreamt, more than once, that I was unclothed with Chandhi next to me, and she was wearing more formal attire. We were walking together through an unfamiliar place, and stepped out, down a step into a more open area. Only later, well after this dream, did we came to discover how the dream's symbolism was intricately part of the Samothracian mythos. But what does that ancient symbolism mean? We have only begun to discover its secrets.

Chapter 4
Witches and Archaic Religion

To more deeply understand ancient Greek religion, we must begin with one of the strangest figures in Greek mythology—Chiron, the centaur. For as it turns out, the mentor of many of the Greek gods and heroes was not, strictly speaking, either a god or a human, but rather Chiron, who brought together three worlds: that of the animals (in particular, horses), that of men, and that of the gods. And doesn't it seem a bit strange that the tutor of so many major figures in Greek mythology was a centaur? The more one looks into this, the more inexplicable it might seem. It is something mostly passed over as yet another peculiarity of Greek mythology. But what I will suggest here in fact provides an explanation. The answer, as it turns out, is intimately bound up with the region (Thessaly, Thrace, and Samothrace) and with magicians and witches. For this whole region was long identified with archaic religion, long into the Greek and then Roman eras.

We should begin, then, with the region itself. The rugged area of northeast Greece bordering the Aegean has long been known as Thessaly, and throughout antiquity was also known for its wildness, for its inhabitants' near-barbarism, and, as a matter of fact, for its witches. Thessaly, Thrace, and Samothrace feature mountains and wilderness—not always tremendous mountains, to be sure (Mount Pelion is more like a long hill fronting the ocean, when one compares it with the Alps), but featuring forests and much wild country even today. In antiquity, when Athens had become the center of what had become the Greek world, already Thessaly had become the northern wild border where witches and magicians were reputed to dwell. It was the home of farming people, among whom continued some of the traditions of archaic religion, especially traditions of medicinal plants, healing, and spells.

In Greek mythology, Asclepius is identified with healing—but where did Asclepius learn the healing arts? In part from his tutor and foster parent Chiron, the centaur, whose home is Mount Pelion. We know of this connection already from Homer's *Iliad,* and know further from Pindar that Chiron was also the teacher of Iasion [Jason], whose very name is said to mean "healer."[25] Asclepius's symbol is a staff up which is entwined a serpent with its head near the top, and this is because he had been given the secrets of healing whispered in his ear by a serpent. In fact, Asclepius was said to be so accomplished at healing that he could bring men back from the dead, but eventually Zeus (it is said) killed him and placed him in the constellation Ophiuchus (the serpent holder).

Now both of these traditions, that of Chiron, and that of Asclepius, have something vital in common: they represent direct connections between Greek and archaic religious traditions. Chiron brings together the animal, human, and divine realms in a distinctively symbolic way—as a centaur, he has the body and legs of a man, but a horse's body and back legs behind. He harks back, in other words, to an archaic shamanic past in which the animal and spirit realms were transparent and accessible. The figure of Chiron is oneiric—he is from a dreamlike twilit world wherein an animal-man conveys sacred spirit-knowledge to heroes and men. This archaic dimension is also visible in the history of the god Poseidon, who in his most archaic version was a god of horsemen and only later was a god of the sea.

Likewise, Asclepius, holding his staff entwined by a serpent, recalls very ancient themes. The serpent (we will recall the rings at Samothrace featured twin serpents) is associated with chthonic knowledge hidden in and under the earth and waters. There is a double aspect to the serpent: on the one hand, it can be venomous and frightening, as symbolized in the myth of the Gorgon or Medusa, but on the other hand, the serpent is also the bearer of secret and healing knowledge. These two aspects are actually complementary, because the secret and sacred knowledge of the serpent is conveyed when one overcomes one's fear of it. The serpent also represents rebirth (the shedding of the snake's skin); hence it corresponds to the rebirth in the Mysteries. The shield of the goddess Athena featured a snake, and her armor featured the severed head of the snake-haired Gorgon because she incorporated into herself the archaic chthonic powers.

Both Chiron the centaur and Asclepius, the healer with the serpent-staff, thus invoke our very archaic and wild human past as overcome by the new gods even as it is continued on among them. Chiron and the centaurs are recalled in the centauromachy panel featured on the Acropolis (in the Parthenon), depicting the battle in mythical antiquity between the Lapith people of the Thessaly region and the half-man, half-horse centaurs. The very presence of the panel, like the figure of Chiron, demonstrates this vital continuity with what the centaurs symbolize. This battle reminds us of the battle between the Titans (the earlier gods) and the new Greek gods, because in both cases, one sees both the subjugation of and the incorporation of the archaic gods into the new pantheon. Likewise, the dangerous and frightening serpent is both subjugated and incorporated as the key source of Asclepius's healing power.

We should also mention the ancient history of the Acropolis in Athens, which also is interwoven with the image of the serpent. Homer remarks that the Acropolis featured a first temple called the "Erechtheion," named for the autochthonous (son of Gaia) first king of Athens, Erechtheus, who was associated with the snake, and indeed, some said he was the same as Cecrops, who was half man, half snake. It is Erechtheus's snake that Athena wears on the inside of her shield. Again, we see here (and in the association of Erechtheus with Poseidon) the invocation of the archaic religious traditions.

While these three figures were male, throughout antiquity the main other associations between magic and Thessaly concerned women, in particular, witches or sorceresses, for which the region was so well known that the very word "Thessalian" widely evoked female practitioners of archaic magic. The most famous association was of Medea, who was Jason's lover in the story of Jason and the Golden Fleece. She was the granddaughter of Helios, the god of the sun in the elder order of the Titans, and represents again the continuity between ancient and newer divinities and traditions. Medea's sorcery made possible the hero Jason's successful journey with the Argonauts; her magic saved him time and again. She was said to be a devotee of Hekate, the goddess of witchcraft, but she is not, in the version of her story told by Apollonius of Rhodes, nearly as monstrous as she was made to be as a tragic literary figure. She was, rather, exemplary of the tradition of witches that worked with herbs and spells in order to change the course of events by saving, healing, or sometimes, killing. Medea became emblematic of the sorceress, and the association between Thessaly and witches reflected that archetype.

Specific to Thessalian witches, it was said, was the art of "drawing down the moon." This trope was mentioned by Plato in his *Gorgias,* but it is by no means clear what exactly "drawing down the moon" really means. There is a comical version, for instance in Aristophanes' *The Clouds,* wherein a character suggests that one might avoid paying a debt by getting a Thessalian witch to draw down the moon, thus keeping the end of the month from coming.[26] But Plato's allusion to this same theme is a bit darker, as Socrates remarks that he would not want to risk what is dearest on acquisition of power, "like those Thessalian enchantresses who, as they say, bring down the moon from heaven at the risk of their perdition."[27]

To what does "drawing down the moon" refer? There is an allusion in Apollonius that Medea's power was to bind the stars and the moon, or a binding power from them, which perhaps makes more sense, since the notion that one physically "pulls down" the moon, as in Aristophanes, of course is a joke. But Medea, Hekate, and sorceresses as well as sorcerers are said to have power in the sublunary realm, that is, they belong to the realm of night, of darkness, of the feminine, of herbs and of caves, and of the crossroads— of what is outside the realm of the sun, the Olympian heights, civilization, the realm of Athenian dialogues and reason. Drawing down the moon, in this context, might be best understood as invoking the powers associated with darkness, and, like Medea, bringing even what appears to be frightening and destructive into the service of the greater good.

One can see that Athens, with its Acropolis and other high points, belongs to the heights, to the sun and sky, but the polytheism of Athens nonetheless had room for the ancient gods and for the gods and goddesses of the night and the underworld. And this inclusivity continued in ancient Rome, where Samothrace and the ancient gods also were honored, and where the reputation of Thessaly and its witches and magicians continued and indeed grew. Among the Roman authors who referred back to the ancient magical spells of Thessalians were Horace, Ovid, Seneca, Lucan, Juvenal, Pliny, and, of course, Apuleius. The Roman authors often depicted the Thessalians as synonymous with not only sorcery but even criminality and evil, as the archaic religions receded even further into the past.

In Apuleius's wonderful novel *The Golden Ass,* he tells the story of Lucius, a randy young man who was the guest of Pamphile, a witch, and her husband, Milo. Lucius relates all manner of amusing and exotic tales, including one of Diophanes, a hapless practitioner of Chaldean astrology, and another of Thelyphron, a student who was once paid for guarding a corpse from the predations of the witches of Thessaly. These witches, he was told, could take any form in order to get access to a corpse: a bird, a mouse, a fly. Nonetheless, he fell into a deep sleep, and for their rituals, the witches cut off hapless Thelyphron's nose and ears rather than those of the corpse—which we later learn because the corpse was resuscitated by an Egyptian initiate and tells the crowd what happened, whereupon Thelyphron's condition (he had been furnished with wax replacements) becomes clear.

But the turning point of the larger narrative occurs when Lucius, who is not only randy but reckless, is literally turned into an ass by the magical unguents of the Thessalian witch Pamphile, supplied by her nubile young servant Photis. Photis takes advantage of poor Lucius, playing humiliating jokes upon him and then suggesting he whip her with a belt to punish her for being bad. Eager to experience Thessalian magic and perhaps be turned into an owl, he has Photis steal an unguent that, far from allowing him to fly, turns him into a miserable beast of burden for the remainder of the novel, which is full of entertaining digressions.

Near the end of the novel, Lucius is saved by the Great Goddess who is associated with the moon, and who goes by many names: Ceres, Venus, Diana, Proserpine, to name but a few. Apuleius presents an enchantingly lovely description of the Goddess rising up out of the sea and revealing herself to the poor ass Lucius. She rises out of the sea with long ringlets of hair, a moon-symbol on her brow, her head encircled by a coronet with serpents on each side, and ears of corn. She wears a multicolored robe and a jet-black cloak, scattered with stars and alive with moonlight. She holds a sistrum, a brass instrument, and a vessel with a handle the shape of a serpent, and she exudes sweet exotic scents.

Lucius is initiated into the great mysteries of the goddess, named in Egypt Isis, and he tells us that he cannot reveal much, only what is lawful to say to the uninitiated. But, he says, he reached and crossed the "gates of death" and saw what is on the other side, in Proserpine's domain. He saw the "sun at midnight," and he "entered the presence of the gods below," as well as "the presence of the gods above." And to all he has been reverent. Seeing the sun at midnight means that duality (day and night, sun and moon) are transcended by his experience; and we should note that he enters "the presence" of the gods, meaning that although there are multiple gods, the divine presence is one.

It is important to note that Apuleius's delightful novel is framed by Thessalian witches early in the narrative proper, and by initiation into the Mysteries of the Great Goddess at the end. They are, in other words, linked. What is more, they are linked by the power of the feminine, either as witch or as goddess, either as seductress or as protectress and savior. And both hark back to archaic religion and to impulses and symbols of untraceable antiquity. The witches correspond to primal impulses, the goddess to transcending those impulses, but the two are linked.

And, we might note, both are emphatically rejected by monotheisms of all stripes.

I am not arguing here that witches are "good"— one has to recognize that the characteristic portrayal in late antiquity is increasingly negative and that much archeological evidence shows widespread use of afflictive or aggressive magic in late antiquity as well as protective magic to avert witchcraft. But the problem is that the more rejected is witchcraft and the ancient religion, the more extreme the dualism enacted in society. Monotheistic or, more accurately, monolatric religions (religions that assert the absolute primacy of one god alone among others) exacerbate this dualism, which results in turn in all kinds of religious pathologies that are not limited to monotheisms, but often seem endemic to them.

Rather, what we find in the archaic religions is holistic in the sense that the goddess and the witch are not excluded but included, even in their more apparently frightening forms. What later became "the devil" in Christianity has many characteristics that belong to earlier archaic European religion. For instance, why does "the devil" have horns, which were characteristic of (for instance) Cernunnos, the Celtic god of fertility and of the underworld whose image is widespread in ancient Brittany and Britain? By contrast, Tibetan Buddhism integrated the archaic religious traditions into it, harnessing them to a higher unity, but this did not happen in the more dualistic monotheistic world. Perhaps only now, as the hegemony of monotheisms wanes, is a more holistic and integrated perspective possible again in European tradition.

The reality is that the sacred and divine cannot properly be understood only in its terms of positive symbols and images like lambs and clouds, because the sacred is power beyond the human, hence beyond also our conventional notions of good and evil. The ancient gods, and we see this in Greek and Roman mythology, as well as in Celtic and Norse religions, do not conform to our human rational constructs, but rather live beyond any conventional bourgeois moral codes, because they ultimately manifest power that is transcendent, even frighteningly so. The paganism that has re-emerged in modern times has not fully come to terms with this, at least as yet. Contemporary paganism also has not fully come to terms with what we may term the invisible realms, or with metaphysics.

Implicit in archaic religion is some transparency between the material and transcendent realms, conveyed through plants, trees, animals, the landscape, mountains, and the sea. The idea is that there are other realms that are sometimes visible through this one. Sometimes those can be glimpsed through sacred trees, animals, or places. Sacredness of place in this world means that what we see or interact with is like a portal. Fire also can be a portal into another, spiritual world, whereby when fire consumes an object, it passes through into another realm. We see this in Vedic *homa* rites, a variant of which were transmitted in Tibetan Buddhism.

In ancient Greek stonework and decoration, including on temples and on graves, one finds stylized eyes. At first, one sees spirals, one opposite another, and then as one looks more closely, one realizes intuitively at first and then consciously, that the spirals and a central pillar are really a stylized face, and the spirals are its eyes. This image, in which the eyes are by virtue of their geometric form a bit eerie, symbolizes eyes that see into another world. The initiate sees or will see life in another world beyond this one; to the initiate, this world is in some sense transparent, and after death one sees the other world. Here the symbolism is not of belief but of direct experience. I include here an image of just such stylized eyes very much akin to those found at Samothrace in the ruins of the temple complex there.

Figure 4-1. Image atop a grave in the ancient cemetery, Athens. Photo by author.

Such images evoke second sight. There are different levels or kinds of seeing, though. One kind is cosmological, which we could also call shamanic—it has to do with the twilight realms, with spirit animals, the psychic, witches, magic or spells. The other is metaphysical, having to do with transcendence and entry into what Plato calls the "islands of the blessed." It is a coincidence neither that Samothrace is an island nor that its Mysteries had two levels. Both of these dimensions, the cosmological and the metaphysical, are present in a complete archaic religion, but as Greco-Roman antiquity waned, the two dimensions separated, so that on the one hand one had the witches, that is the cosmological and shamanic dimension, which was feared and then suppressed and rejected by confessional Christianity; and on the other hand one had the mysticism of transcendence that was continued, sometimes carried along in the margins of confessional Christianity as apophatic mysticism like that of Dionysius the Areopagite.[28]

In other words, the archaic Mysteries continued into Greek and then Roman mythology in late antiquity, where although different gods and god-names arose, the Mysteries of Samothrace were still preserved in their ancient tongue. But one could argue that aspects of the Mysteries continued even into Christendom, and indeed, continued all the way through the modern era, albeit in different forms, sometimes deemed heretical, sometimes not. Of course, the Mysteries themselves were no longer celebrated at Samothrace with the ascent of confessional Christianity, and indeed, over time the entire temple complex was laid waste by both man and nature. Before we delve deeper into some important aspects of the Mysteries and Samothrace, though, we need to look more closely at the new gods, and what they still have to tell us.

Chapter 5
Coming to Know the Gods

I had been to Athens before, but hadn't gone to the Acropolis. I'm not sure why—perhaps it wasn't time to do so yet. In the meantime, I had been to countless sacred sites in North America, in Western Europe, and in Western England. I had been to megaliths, dolmens, petroglyphs in the high desert of New Mexico, terraglyphs in the Great Plains, all manner of sacred places. Perhaps visiting those other places prepared me in some ways, but whatever the reason, just before we went to Samothrace, I went on a pilgrimage to the Acropolis, that extraordinary citadel above the sprawling city of Athens. To go to such a place, to truly go there, not as a tourist but as a participant, open to what is really there, is to be exalted. I was astonished, for it was on the Acropolis that I began to become aware of the presence of the gods, intimations of what it is to know them.

The   ascent up to the Acropolis, in the bright sunshine, under the philosophers' trees, is circuitous, and one is always accompanied by others, coming and going. I do not know what their experience might be. As one crosses over onto the marble outcropping itself—the vast, teeming city of Athens spread out below one, in the distance the other outcrops, including Lycabettus Hill—one feels oneself alone, just you, the marble below, and the cerulean sky above, bounded by the horizon. To be on the Acropolis is itself exaltation; one feels exalted just to be on such a place on such a day, nearby the magnificence of the great Parthenon and the temples, including the most recent one to the right, the newest temple of Athena, patroness of the city and the region.

The Parthenon is, of course, world-renowned, but it is the high marble rocky outcrop itself, above the city, that is exalting; the Parthenon participates in and emblematizes this exaltation. Sacred sites, both in North America and in Europe, tend to have common characteristics: height, directional orientation, water, stone(s), all are signs, and when they appear together, it is an archaic sacred site. The Acropolis, it might seem, does not have water, or so one would think standing high above the city, with the breeze blowing in around one from the sea. And of course, a dozen miles or so further there is the sea, and for that matter, Eleusis near it, home to the ancient Mysteries of the Athens region. But, it is said, there is a sacred spring hidden away even today atop the marble hill, and, I was told, the water still flows there.

Plato, in his *Cratylus,* gives us some clues about Athena, whose high outcrop this is. Plato tells us that interpreters of Homer say that her name derives from *theou noesis* (θεοῦ νόησις), which means *noesis* [participatory intelligence or knowing] of the divine presence [*theou*]. This become Etheonoe, which evokes also *en ethei noesin* [moral intelligence], and, Plato adds, was eventually altered into the form we know, Athene or Athena.[29] Thus, Athena, and her temples at the top of the Acropolis, is the point of participation in the noetic intelligence of the gods; she is also the fierce protector of that intelligence's presence, with her warrior visage and sword.

We already saw that Athena has the symbolism of the slain snake-headed Gorgon on her shield, as well as that of the ancient serpent on the inside, but she also is associated with the owl and its wings, and she is known as *glaukopis,* or "the one with gleaming eyes." And of course she is identified with the olive tree, because of the myth that she and Poseidon vied for patronage of Athens, but she won with an olive tree, the most valuable of gifts to the Greeks. With all of these ancient symbols, including the sacred tree, we see behind and embodied in the iconography of Athena truly archaic animal and plant symbols, not to mention her "bright eyes" that see far into different worlds at once.

Thus the goddess Athena has to be understood not only in terms of mythological narratives but also in terms of the deeply archaic symbolism that we saw manifested at Samothrace. Although there are myths about Athena, what I came to realize, as I was standing atop the Acropolis on that sunny June afternoon, is that the myths convey clues about how to understand her, but they are only clues. Atop that high outcrop, among her temples' high pillars where she sits enthroned, it is not in the myths but in the place itself that one feels the presence of the divine. I experienced an indescribable spiritual elevation that is inseparable from the actual climb to the heights of the Acropolis itself. Perhaps not for everyone, but at least for me, to be atop the Acropolis then was to begin to know Athena not as a figure but as a presence.

Here the word "know" has different dimensions than we might ordinarily recognize in it. What I realized is that although we can discursively know the details of Athena's dress, or of the relationship between her and Athens, or of her and warfare, there is a second level of such knowledge that is intuitive, in which the symbolism of the goddess gives indications of her particular associations and qualities, and a third level that we might call recognition, but which the Platonists would call "theurgy," meaning a kind of direct familiarity, communication, or exchange with the deity.

When it comes to Samothrace, though, a different set of myths provides continuity with archaic religion, a collection of hints and associations that convey a great deal in indirect ways. Here we refer to the constellations of Greek and Roman myths of Demeter and Persephone, Hekate, Dionysus, Bacchus, and others. Earlier, we saw how the mythology of Jason and the Argonauts was tied in to Samothrace in a number of ways, not least, that they were initiated at Samothrace and that Jason was responsible for the opening of the Mysteries to all who were worthy. But what connections were there between the Mysteries of the Great Gods and the Greco-Roman mythological cycles?

In addition to Dionysus and Orpheus, the primary Greco-Roman mythological figures associated with the Mysteries at Samothrace were Hades, who rules the Underworld; Persephone, Queen of the Underworld; Hekate, daughter of the Titans, who ruled night, witchcraft, magic, sorcery, herbs, spells; Demeter and Ceres, who were associated with the agricultural cycles and the mysteries of fertility and of crops; the Korybantes or band of warriors in service to the Great Mother; Kadmilos, an ithyphallic god associated with Hermes, the messenger of the gods; the Celestial Twins, Dardanos and Aetion, associated with the Dioscuri, or Castor and Pollux; and finally, the myth of Cadmus [Kadmilos] and Harmonia [Elektra], a divine couple whose wedding enacts the *hieros gamos* or transcendent marriage.

This is, of course, an extraordinarily rich, diverse set of myths that, when bundled together, present no immediately clear pattern but rather seem surprisingly heterogenous. How to make sense of all of them? What would so many different myths tell us about the Mysteries of Samothrace? Or are they so many disparate, subsequent, more or less extraneous accretions to the archaic tradition by Greek and Roman historians or Christian opponents of the ancient Mysteries? One argument is indeed that all these later myths and associations do not really reveal much about the ancient Mysteries of the Great Gods, but rather obscure them, and are something to be swept aside. However, to sweep them aside would be to ignore how ancient mythology worked associatively. To better understand how mythology worked, we might begin by looking at the larger mythological patterns in these different myths and mythological cycles.

One dominant mythos among these that ties a number of these figures is that of Persephone. Of course, there are different versions of the myth of Persephone or in Latin, Proserpine. In the most well-known version, Persephone was carried off by Hades, the Underworld King, and her distraught mother Demeter—whose grief made the earth barren and who was guided by Hekate—searched for and eventually found her daughter in the Underworld. Persephone, however, had eaten the seeds of a pomegranate down below, which bound her to the Underworld for four months of the year, and this is the explanation for why we have the winter season during which the earth is barren. That there is a connection to Samothrace is clear because the harbor (such as it was) had the name in antiquity, Demetrium.[30]

Now the myth of Persephone, or Proserpine, was in fact associated with Samothrace by many ancients. But what were the esoteric implications of this myth? Arguably the greatest of the German philosophers, Friedrich Wilhelm Joseph Schelling, developed a comprehensive theory of mythology whose foundation was his initial extended analysis of Samothrace and its mythology.[31] Schelling's analysis of Samothracian mythology is too extensive to go into here, except for the following, relevant to our current discussion. Schelling observes that contrary to conventional interpretations of the Samothracian theology, it is in fact an ascending series of deities. The lowest of these is Demeter or Ceres, "whose essence is hunger and seeking." She is the "remotest origin" of actual being. The next is Proserpine, who is the essence or fundamental origin of the whole visible external natural world. Then comes Dionysus, Lord of the spirit world. And above both nature and spirit world is Kadmilos, or Hermes, who mediates between the others and transcendence above them. Thus, Schelling writes, "the Cabiri doctrine was a system ascending from subordinate personalities of nature deities" up to "a transcendent god."[32]

Later Schelling goes on to explain the nature of this ascendant order in more detail. He remarks that "the first Cabiri were magical or, to speak more precisely, theurgic, those powers or natures bringing the higher gods to realization." They do not do this individually, but as part of a "magical chain binding the lowest with the highest." Just as the Dioscuri must appear as two paired lights, so too the Cabiri all must appear together; they are united magically, and so initiation into the mysteries had the effect of binding one to the higher gods beyond life and death. The initiate "becomes a link of that magical chain, himself a Kabir, taken up into the unbreakable relation" and joined to the chorus of the higher gods who are symbolized in the dance of the stars in the night sky. This is, Schelling observes, an indestructible set of ideas from the remotest primitive times, and "of all paganism, is the purest and closest to the truth."[33]

But how does the mythology associated with these figures reflect the Mysteries of Samothrace? The myth of Persephone/Proserpine is one of death and rebirth. She goes into the Underworld and becomes its Queen, but she also returns to nature and to this world, which she revivifies. And her rebirth, that is, her return, is due to the assistance of Hekate, queen of the spirits. One of Persephone's names is Kore (the maiden), and one of her epithets is *Kore Soteira,* that is, the salvific maiden, she who saves. Persephone, in turn, is said to be the mother of the god Dionysus, whose father was Zeus. Dionysus Zagreus was thereby said, in Orphic tradition, to present a salvific and liberating power (one of his epithets was Eleutherios, he who makes free). He was said to be the last of the gods accepted into the Olympian deities; and he mediates between the natural and the spirit worlds. Finally, there is Hermes, messenger of the gods, whose herm-pillars featured an erect phallus.

What meanings can we draw from all of these mythological associations? First, we know that the Mysteries both at Samothrace and Eleusis were associated with Demeter and Persephone, in the case of Samothrace, by syncrasis, or joining together later and earlier mythologies. For instance, we know that there was an association at Samothrace with ithyphallic male gods; that association could be conjoined with the ithyphallic Dionysos or Hermes. Second, we know that there was a salvific dimension to both Mystery centers; Samothrace was renowned for saving mariners. Third, we know there was held to be a posthumous dimension to the Eleusinian Mysteries, and have seen that there also was held to be such a dimension to the Samothracian Mysteries. Fourth, we know that there were indeed magical and theurgic aspects, particularly of the Samothracian Mysteries.

It is confusing, however, to see arrayed all of these associated gods and goddesses and mythologies at Samothrace. All of these different names and associations—what to make of them all? There were the original Samothracian deities' names, Axieros, Axiokersa, Axiokersos, Kasmilos, and then there were the Greek deities associated with them, followed by the Roman names superimposed on those. A monotheistic interpretation is to project back into polytheism a single god behind the other gods—with the corollary that polytheism is "evolving" toward monotheism. But Schelling proposed an alternative interpretation.

What we find in the classical sources are exoteric allusions to the Mysteries, and the association of different deities with them is also exoteric, whereas the Mysteries themselves are by definition esoteric.

In this context, esoteric has multiple implications: it is experiential, in that the Mysteries were conveyed through ritual enactment; and it is metaphysical, in that through ritual enactment, the initiate experiences progressively deeper insights into the nature of particular deities and ultimately into that which transcends particular deities. Thus, Mystery rituals introduced initiates to a series of glimpses into Demeter's loss and recovery of Persephone, and the salvific emergence from the Underworld of Kore Soteira. Through spiritual drama, the initiate is purified, undergoing a catharsis like that alluded to be Aristotle (but only there in secular terms), here in its original spiritual form as induced crisis and salvific resolution.

Behind or beyond the drama is a metaphysical process, the progressive revelation of the Absolute that transcends all dichotomies. Schelling wrote about this revelation as "a kind of cognition that is not added to the soul through instruction, teaching, etc."—that is, it does not come through external means or discursive reason—but rather, is intuitive direct cognition that goes beyond the body and the world of the senses or appearances to "the originary [Ursprüngliche] state."[34] All philosophical instruction pointing to this state must be in the form of negation; it is the primordial intuition of the transcendence of duality, that is, of subject and object as separate. The Mysteries, in other words, were ultimately about guiding or showing initiates their own identity with the transcendence of self and other.

Unfortunately, Schelling continued, those who do not recognize this truth often engage in polemics about it, precisely because they have not made any real advances in philosophy and thus "can only express themselves through notions of reflective cognition."[35] And this observation by Schelling, made in 1804, proved to be prophetic. For Schelling's insights indeed were attacked by many of his fellow philosophers of the time, who clung to reflective or discursive cognition. Hence Hegel, in a polemic primarily directed against Schelling, scoffed that in such an intuitive cognition of transcendence, "all cows are black." But in fact Schelling was deeply steeped in literature of the ancient Mysteries, as well as in the theosophy of Jacob Böhme, and understood them much more deeply than his opponents.

What Schelling realized was that embedded in the Mysteries was the revelation of the various deities, celebrated exoterically in mythologies conveyed through hymns, poetry and drama, as all emerging from and guiding the initiate toward their own transcendent nature, which he termed the Absolute. Thus ancient paganism externally was polytheistic, but esoterically or inwardly was not because the various deities were expressions of the Absolute. The initiate through direct intuition is able to realize the "true, beautiful, and good in itself" which "can be symbolized in temporal terms as the pre-existence of the soul."[36] In other words, the initiate glimpses what transcends time. From a temporal perspective, this glimpse is of eternity, meaning that the individual experiences or sees what transcends the limited temporal self that is born and dies.

This intuitive direct cognition of transcendence is accompanied by the withdrawal from the body and emotional reactivity; it means the soul's convalescence from the primal illness of immersion in the sensate life [*Sinnenleben*] and resultant emotional turbulence of attachment and aversion. In place of this mental and emotional turbulence comes direct perception of the true, beautiful, and good, which is eternal or in eternity, that is, not subject to temporal or spatial limitation.[37] Those religious impulses that derive from dualism and infatuation with the sensory world, the body, and self—betrayed by seeking dominion over others or violence—are entirely contrary to this kind of spiritual process. This process, Schelling observes, is for those who "penetrate the [exoteric] shell" to reach the inner or esoteric meaning of religious symbolism and who prove themselves through moderation, self-conquest, devotion to transcendence, and wisdom to become "adepts, who see the truth as it is, without the mediation of images."[38]

Where did Schelling come to these insights concerning the Mysteries? He was steeped in the work of the Platonists, first of all. What he writes here is fundamentally Platonic, but there is a long history of connections between the Platonic tradition and the Mysteries, beginning with Plato himself, who directly refers to them and to what it means to be an initiate. Philosophy, in this Platonic tradition, is an exposition of what is fundamentally a spiritual process, the purpose of which is to gain direct knowledge of the divine and to become a good and wise person, to realize truth for ourselves. Philosophy is not merely discursive; it is, rather, a discursive exposition of an inner or esoteric process leading to direct insight into timelessness and transcendence of the limited or apparent self.

And now we come to a subject I have not seen discussed elsewhere: the hidden relationship between Christianity and the Mystery traditions. Because so many of the Church Fathers, as they are known, expressed bitter denunciations of the ancient Greek pagan traditions and of the Mysteries, we might think that there could be no real continuity between Christianity and the earlier Mysteries. And indeed, a good case can be made that confessional Christianity—that is, the forms of Christianity predicated on belief alone—was and still is the mortal enemy of any and all gnostic traditions, of Platonism, of Hermetism, of the Mystery traditions. Certainly that is the impression given by the vitriolic ridicule of figures like Tertullian and Irenaeus.

And yet there are some interesting aspects of the early Christian tradition that might deserve at least a bit of recognition. The first of these came to me when I was standing atop the Acropolis above Athens. Down below, one can see a smaller reddish marble outcropping, more or less in the shadow of the mighty Acropolis. That reddish outcropping is known as the Areopagus, that is, the red stone of the warrior god

Ares. But it is also the namesake of Dionysius the Areopagite, the first disciple of Paul, who reputedly preached here when he came to Athens. And the most essential early Christian author for subsequent Christian mysticism also has the name Dionysius the Areopagite.

Just to be clear: this means that early Christianity and the seminal figure of Paul is directly linked to the Acropolis, and that what is more, so too is the most important figure for mysticism in early Christianity, the mysterious author of *Mystical Theology* and other treatises that shaped the entire subsequent history of Christian mysticism. But there turn out to be more such links. Paul is well known for his letters to different communities of Christians, and among those the Corinthians are the most prominent. Ancient Corinth had its own sacred outcropping, the Acrocorinth, with a sacred spring, the Upper Peirene, and played a role in the saga of Jason and the Argonauts. It is not far from Delphi, where the famous oracle and the temple of Apollo were situated. Further, when he was traveling, at one point Paul is said to have stayed on the island of Samothrace. And as is widely noted, Paul refers to the "mystery" and the "mysteries" of Christianity. Without any doubt, Paul moved through a sociocultural landscape suffused by the ancient Mysteries.

But one could go either way in interpreting this. After all, it is hard to forget the moving images, in the Museum near the Acropolis today, depicting tiny early Christians assiduously toppling the magnificent

Greek images adorning the temples atop the Acropolis, industriously destroying the most beautiful statues in the world. Surely the followers of monotheistic confessionalism couldn't have been carrying on the ancient Mysteries at the same time that they were earnestly ruining the ancient sacred places! And yet, there is an alternative way of understanding the confluence of the ancient Mysteries and Christianity, provided by an old friend deeply immersed in the Christian mysteries.

There are, he told me, fundamentally two different types of Christianity. One is the kind that results in the fundamentalism visible in the destruction of the ancient temples and statues, and much later, in the destruction of standing stones in Britain. It is anti-mystical and creed-based, demanding blind faith or belief; it is doctrinaire; it is hostile to viewpoints other than its own, especially to esoteric or pagan perspectives. But the other kind of Christianity is much more mysterious. This second type of Christianity is alive in Eastern forms of the tradition, particularly in Greek Orthodoxy, which can be likened to a conveyor of electrical current. To encounter it is to experience the *mysterion,* which cannot be described, but which is conveyed in the images and liturgy and living presence of the Church itself. This other kind of Christianity is fundamentally a mystery religion, celebrating the revelatory and salvific power of the Christos, the light.

To this second type of Christianity belong two broad groups or currents. One, in Greek and more broadly in Eastern forms of Christianity, includes mysticism, particularly what is known as hesychastic mysticism. Of course, in modernity, Eastern Christianity has tended to de-emphasize its mystical heritage, but it still exists. The other broad group, in Western European forms of Christianity, represents the continuity of apophatic Platonic mysticism. This tradition harks back to the works of Dionysius the Areopagite as well as to Clement of Alexandria and Origen, and includes many major figures, among whom we might list John Scotus Eriugena, Meister Eckhart, Johannes Tauler, Marguerite of Porete, Nicholas of Cusa, and to some extent, Jacob Böhme.

What my friend suggests, in other words, is that the heart of the ancient Mystery tradition was conveyed in some limited respects into Christianity in two different ways.[39] In one way, we see the celebration of Christian liturgical mysteries, which in his view are to be understood as manifesting the Christian Mystery revelation of Christos, the divine light. And in the other way, we see the continuation in Christianity of the earlier Platonic mystical tradition of sheer apophatic transcendence that, he argues, comes through the Mysteries into Platonism, and from Platonism into Christianity.

Of course, at this point one might interject a clarification. Some claim that Platonism is monotheistic, or at least compatible with monotheism as usually understood in confessional forms of Christianity. And it is true that Plotinus, for instance, refers to the ascent toward realizing god. But what sort of god? The Plotinian god is clearly not the jealous tribal deity of Old Testament Judaism, self-described as a "jealous god" and seen commanding murders of competing tribes and desecration of others' tribal lands. Rather, the Plotinian god is metaphysically one, the dawn of absolute transcendence of self and other. Thus Platonism is not monotheism, or monolatry, that is, the worship of one tribal god among others.

Rather, Platonic mysticism recognizes multiple deities, but at the same time acknowledges the fundamental unity of the divine presence. In some respects, this is akin to Vajrayana Buddhism, in which there are myriad Buddhas, deities, dakinis and herukas, but nonetheless Buddhist metaphysics cannot properly be described as dualistic in any way, because ultimate reality is beyond dualities and beyond conceptual constructs. As I've shown in *Perennial Philosophy,* the Platonic tradition is analogous to Buddhism in this regard.[40]

One could in fact best understand the Christian Mystery, my friend said, not in terms of belief or faith, which seen in those terms is hopelessly dualistic, but rather in the larger context of the ancient Mysteries. Christianity—in what is truly important about it— is a process of initiation and illumination; and illumination is come to through the process described in the Platonic tradition, the same process that belonged to the ancient Mysteries before Platonism. This is, of course, a new way of seeing Christianity, not as an alien tribal overlay atop indigenous European traditions but rather as a continuation of them in a new way.

There is a revealing passage attributed by some to Plutarch about the Mysteries that may help us to understand more clearly this point. In this passage, we find the following:

> Thus death (*teleutan*, literally, the end of life) and initiation (*teleisthai*) closely correspond; even the words correspond, and so do the things. At first there are wanderings, and toilsome running about in circles and journeys through the dark over uncertain roads and culs de sac; then, just before the end, there are all kinds of terrors, with shivering, trembling, sweating, and utter amazement. After this, a strange and wonderful light meets the wanderer; he is admitted into clean and verdant meadows, where he discerns gentle voices, and choric dances, and the majesty of holy sounds and sacred visions. Here the now fully initiated is free, and walks at liberty like a crowned and dedicated victim, joining in the revelry; he is the companion of pure and holy men, and looks down upon the uninitiated and unpurified crowd here below in the mud and fog, trampling itself down and crowded together, though of death remaining still sunk in its evils, unable to believe in the blessings that lie beyond. That the wedding and close union of the soul with the body is a thing really contrary to nature may clearly be seen from all this.[41]

There is no mention here of particular deities—rather, the initiate enters into divine presence and light and is deified. *This* is what is meant by "coming to know the gods."

In *Gorgias,* Socrates discusses the law of heaven that still exists from the time of the Titans until now, in which the good go after death to the "Islands of the Blessed" and the unvirtuous go to Tartarus to receive their just penalty. The uninitiated, Socrates memorably says, are like a colander, full of holes and leaky, whereas the initiate is like a sealed-up vessel. That is what we see, in a different way, in the description of initiation into the Mysteries that was preserved by Stobaeus and has been attributed to Plutarch. The initiate passes through terror and confusion, and then divine light dawns, and he is admitted into the light, into verdant meadows, and sees sacred visions. The individual is, to use Socrates' term, "sealed," and no longer for this time subject to mental and physical suffering; he has gone to the "Islands of the Blessed."

In this context, the labels are perhaps not as important as the process itself. What matters is the experiential process, the "sealing" of the human vessel through the process of initiation that ensures the individual is morally upright, a better person, able therefore to experience what Schelling describes this way: it "appears before the soul only at the moment when subjective activity joins the objective in unexpected harmony" and manifests itself as "happiness, as illumination, or as revelation."[42] This illuminating experience of the Absolute is above religious dogmatism, beyond faith and reason, because it is the direct and serene cognition of what transcends the human.

Thus what is essential about coming to know the gods is not inherently polytheistic, nor is it theistic— it is, rather, the individual process of initiation, that is, of dying before death, and resurrection into the light and the empyrean. The "Islands of the Blessed" belong to those who find their way there or who are shown them, whatever faith tradition one putatively belongs to. This is why the Mysteries at Samothrace were open to all comers, as long as they passed the inquiry at the portal. Coming to know the gods means that one becomes godlike oneself; one's own divinity becomes clear. And as a result of this revelation and clarification, the very earth itself is revealed to be of a different substance. What such a revelation means, we will examine in our next chapter, when we look at the ancient stones.

Chapter 6
The Stones

The first thing one notices, at the Sanctuary of the Great Gods, is the stones, piled higgledy-piggledy along the entryway path, everywhere long pillars and base stones, the remains of what once must have been a magnificent temple complex here, now completely broken apart and in ruins. Stones are scattered everywhere, and when we were there, archaeologist-directed crews were industriously moving some larger remains hither and yon with heavy equipment and wooden pallets, as if the destruction of millennia was not enough, as if every bit of the past needed to be manhandled, piled, moved, catalogued, and, were it possible, still more profaned. What to make of the scattered stones of the sanctuary?

I could begin by remarking that I've traveled many thousands of miles to visit different sacred sites, across North America, in England, in Brittany, in Switzerland, and of course in Greece. I have been to countless standing stones, to high rock outcroppings in different cities, on sacred plateaus in the wilderness, to Tintagel, the birthplace of the Arthurian legends, so I have come to recognize many aspects of sacred sites that one might ordinarily miss. And as we stood amid the ruins of the *Hieron* of the Sanctuary of the Great Gods, I could sense and see aspects of the stones around us that contributed much to this sacred place.

I recalled being among the menhirs and dolmens of Brittany. The word "menhir"—*maen hir* or "long stone" in Breton—refers to something really quite mysterious, for throughout the region along the Western coast one finds standing stones, and not just alone, but sometimes in great phalanxes of not just hundreds but thousands that go over hills and along the curve of the land. In the forest, I glimpsed a telltale vertical grey that marked a *menhir*. Walking into the forest, one realizes that one is standing in a processional array of standing stones, ahead many others, in stately silence for millennia among the slowly growing younger trees.

This was the *Petit-Ménec,* an array of standing stones not too far from the much larger and more widely known array at Carnac. The trees were themselves like younger watchers among the ancient standing stones, which were aligned in a kind of L shape, first the processional way, then to the right or southwest toward the ocean. The stones were mossy-green on their northern side, and each was distinctive, yet each was the same grey surface, speckled with flecks of quartz. Putting one's hand on them, one could feel the millennia in them as sentinels here.

Human civilizations rise and fall, great wars rage, and still they stand.

And what is their purpose? Why would the ancients have expended so much effort and time to place these thousands of stones in such precise rows and with such care that they stand for thousands of years past and will stand for thousands more into the future? What is their *meaning?* We have no sure way of knowing through academic research; there are no texts; there is no manual; the stones are their own inscrutable explanation of themselves, resistant to the calculative mind. Standing in the midst of the thousands of standing stones of Kermario, Menec, and Kerlescan, one can see why there is a legend that the stones were Roman legions frozen by the magic of Merlin—but that hardly explains them.

And it was here that I first began to notice another key to the stones: their directional orientation, often, at least partly aligned toward the southwest or south-southwest. What might that direction mean? Does the directional orientation correspond to some constellation, or to the rising or setting of the sun or moon? Or is it a metaphysical orientation? In Celtic tradition—and Brittany is one of the last redoubts of Celtic culture—West is associated with the Otherworld and with sacred knowledge. Furthermore, the West is held to be where the sacred day begins—in fact, Julius Caesar remarked about the Celts that they counted not days, but nights for this very reason. So going into the West and into the setting sun is actually moving toward the beginning and the new day after the night. The circle (moving deosil) begins in the West, then goes to the North, symbolizing conflict or struggle, then to the East, symbolizing prosperity, flowering, brightness, and then the South, growth, warmth, and cultural life as well as death. Finally, we return to the West, the most mysterious of directions, encompassing beginning and end, life and death, the portal between this world and the Otherworld.[43]

I remember traveling to the Gulf of Morbihan, to the very tip of the Quiberon peninsula. There, the ocean breeze whips the black rocky edge of the Côte Sauvage, where the standing stones have stood as sentinels over the sea for millennia. I wondered whether it was iron oxide in the rock shelf there, because the compass spun misleadingly when I stood near some of the menhirs on the high grassy knolls. It is a desolate region, this wild coast; there, one looks out to sea over much the same vista one would have seen four or five thousand years before.

It was atop the dolmen *Les Pierres Plates* that I began to consider whether the standing stones of the entire region might be connected. Across the bay of Quiberon was the island Gavrinis with its ancient pagan sanctuary whose dolmen has a carving that pairs with one on the mainland dolmen at *Table des Marchande*s, showing a bull and a pair of axes. Here, the dolmen looks out on an angle toward the sea, in front of it a menhir whose surface is as craggy as a corrugated tree trunk. I wondered if the single menhir, which one often finds near a passage entrance, serves to conduct power that the dolmen passage then grounds. Or perhaps the menhir serves as a kind of radiating antenna from the passageway out.

From above, the dolmen's long series of stones formed a kind of processional runway toward the ocean, and some of the topstones were carved with a distinctive series of lines, as if to mark how power was conducted one way or another. Inside, the passageway was long and dark; one has to squat to move through it, and the walls are carved with labyrinthine engravings into the stone that some think are heralds of a mother goddess. But it is hard to discern what precisely these symmetrical engravings might mean, any more than we can be certain why there are lines engraved in the stones above us. Perhaps these are sigils taken from the realm of Ideas and made visible in the place to which they belong and that manifests them.

Here, at this desolate, windswept, stone-marked knoll, surrounded by small yellow flowers, the ocean sparkling in the distance, we began to wonder if all these stones could be seen from above as a grand sigil, a pattern from heaven laid out upon the land and sea. I stood where the creators of this dolmen stood, seeing now what they saw then, more than five thousand years before. Their stones bore the marks of eternity; touching them, we are touching stones in time, but also what is beyond time.

I was not the first to think all these sites were somehow linked. The indefatigable Alexander Thom and his son proposed in *Megalithic Remains in Britain and Brittany* that when plotted on a large map of the region, the major standing stones, dolmens, and sacred sites of Brittany are on a northeast/southwest axis, centered in Le Grande Menhir Brisé and running outward in a starlike pattern, one ray going from the central menhir up toward Petit-Ménec and Le Moustoir, another ray southwest (left) toward the alignments and stones below Saint-Pierre, another heading further down toward the stones and dolmens of South Quiberon, still another ray toward Petit Mont to the southeast, and yet another up (right) toward Travas in the east.[44]

Standing atop the ancient dolmen on the southwestern tip of Quiberon peninsula, it certainly seemed to me that these thousands and thousands of stones embedded in the earth across this region were connected and formed larger patterns in Western France of significance for all of Western Europe. These stones stood untouched and pristine, reminders of archaic Europe, one could also say, of primordial Europe and of primordial Europeans. But what were their purposes? They were ciphers whose key eluded us in the modern world.

With the precision of his engineer's training, Alexander Thom calculated the alignments of standing stones with regard to the cycles of the moon and the summer and winter solstices. And others have suggested that there may be connections between some of the standing stones and the movement of particular constellations in the night sky; and others have sought to connect the stones with agricultural cycles; and still others have seen them as geometrical patterns whose origin is best understood as a variant of Pythagorean and Platonic mathematics.

Of the latter group, the finest author is undoubtedly John Michell, whom I had visited in London in his peculiarly vertical flat there. I remember traipsing up stairs with him from one book-and-paper-crowded floor to the next. John had concluded that the standing stones represent what he called "megalithic science," in which the stones are the "instruments." This megalithic science was based upon Pythagorean mathematics and practiced by "the philosopher-priests of remote antiquity."[45] Of particular interest, he said, is "the relation between the earth and sky, bride and bridegroom in the mythological sacred marriage." The phallic menhir and the earth-womb of the dolmen—these are, he thought, "symbols of the sacred union and the instruments of its consummation." The purpose of the megalithic science, he said, is to stimulate the process whereby the cosmic and solar energy fertilizes the spirit of the earth.

Was this indeed the key to the great stones of antiquity? Even today, there remain folk traditions about the megaliths and fertility. In Brittany and Britain alike, certain stones are held to be particularly strong in their magic; and even after more than a millennia and a half of Christian interdiction, the oral tradition continues in Bretagne of stones that will increase a woman's fertility and a man's virility. But these stones were not placed just anywhere; they marked telluric currents, places of terrestrial magnetism, where, when placed there, the stones became conductors. The megalithic science was also an art, and the name for both art and science is magic.

How did the stones of the ancient Samothracian sanctuary reflect such an art and a science? We saw every manner of stone there at Samothrace, an extraordinary variety of them, here all concentrated into a single place. There were volcanic stones, quartz-flecked stones, marble, magnetized stones, grey stones, white stones, black stones, red stones— tall pillars and the remains of carved lintels, stone steps, stone amphitheater. The valley next to the mountain, looking out to the Aegean Sea, had every kind of sacred stone in it that I have ever seen in other sites in Europe, but here were brought together to form an extraordinary temple complex.

Why are the stones themselves important? In such a place, they are imbued with the power of the place. If the sanctuary was home to theurgic power, as it was so long reputed to have been, then that power was retained in the very stones themselves. Perhaps this was why those who came later, the confessional monotheists, took it upon themselves to tear apart every stone, to leave behind only the ruins on the ground of what once was a magnificent, royally endowed sacred place, adorned with delicate Greek statuary, with the most famous statue of antiquity, the Nike spirited away by a marauding party to decorate a staircase in Paris. Of course, the place itself had power, but the stones were there to augment its power.

And the destruction of the place, accomplished by nature through earthquakes, by pirates, and by religious zealots, was not complete. As soon as one arrives in such a place, one can sense that here there still is what once was, that if a portal is opened to eternity, then eternity is still there, and it cannot be otherwise. There is a power in these sacred places, and at Samothrace it is palpable, that cannot be extinguished; it is simply there, just as if an electric line is "live," it carries electrical current. And one cannot say that electrical current in itself is either "good" or "bad"; it is neither all sweetness and light nor darkness, but more like a conductor-point of power. It still is.

The power of pilgrimage to sacred sites relies not just upon the site itself but also, and even more, upon the prior transmutation of the pilgrim. One has to be morally prepared for the initiation, the ancients said—to be initiated, one had to answer the question what was the worst thing one had done. The purpose of pilgrimage to a sacred site is in the pilgrimage itself, which is also an initiation. No such site is easy to get to—all, and especially Samothrace, a remote island in the Aegean, require one to travel for days, over land and water, to arrive there. One has to purify oneself; one has to be open before the sacred site can work its magic. And the sacred site alone is also not enough; for beyond the pilgrimage itself, one needs those who are caretakers, who preserve the culture of initiatic transmission, the ancient sacred language and traditions. Everything, at such a place, must converge for initiation to take place.

The power of the stones is to preserve; they both store and convey. If the theurgic praxis at a sacred place is powerful enough, perhaps it could be embedded in the very stones themselves. And the presence of so many different kinds of stones would serve to store and convey all the different aspects of that praxis. The stones are materiality, but materiality can be penetrated to its depths by spiritual power; the initiative life of the place is preserved here, like memories are preserved in the materiality of the brain, traces of light in the depths.

But we live in a time when no such power is acknowledged, and while many of the sacred places of indigenous Europe are preserved, no one wants to acknowledge what those sacred places are for, or what they mean. The standing stones of Carnac still stand, the dolmens still look out over the ocean, the stones of Samothrace are still in the earth there, but who today knows or wants to know what such things mean? And if no one knows or cares, do the Mysteries survive at all? They may survive, not only in the traces of them that we possess among the classical authors, not only in the stones themselves, but also in their more intangible but nonetheless real role in human cultural life as enduring portals to the Islands of the Blessed.

I thought, for the first time, standing in Samothrace, that in some pagan renaissance of the future, the temple complex here could be restored, renewed. What once was might be again. After all, the landscape itself, the elements that made this a sacred place many thousands of years ago are still here; if you stand on the floorstones of the Hieron, you still look out over the Aegean to the sacred north. Would it be possible to restore this place, to return to it the aspects of human culture that enlivened it for millennia? Surely it is not impossible. But what is lacking is the culture that gives the place and its rituals meaning and power.

To think that such a renewal is possible is to recognize not only the enduring power of such a place but, even more, what such a place represents as being both in and yet not of time. For in the end, that is what makes a site truly sacred. It belongs to nature, it is true; it is recognized by the human world of culture; this too is true. But beyond these and beyond the enduring markers of such places, which are rare, is something intangible. It is as intangible as the magnetic power of some stones, or of the far north, but it is nonetheless real. And it is to the kinds of magnetism, and their meaning, that we now turn.

Chapter 7
Magnetism

The two of us stood behind the Hieron among the ruins of the great temple complex at Samothrace, looking at a compass that I held outstretched between us. The pointer swiveled when we walked forward and moved due north, but when we stepped back, it moved back to north-northwest. "Why do you suppose it does that?" I asked Chandhi. "It's definitely changing what's due north, but only here," she replied. "It means that this part of the complex is *always* oriented exactly north, even when over the millennia north, and the pole star, has changed." It was only later that we came to think that the magnetic orientation guiding the compass might not be only the magnetic north, that "north" might in fact be determined more permanently here by lodestones embedded in the earth.

It is the case that north of the Hieron—near the largest enclosed circular structure known in the Greek world—is a half-buried grayish red-purple color of porphyritic boulder, the stone of royalty. This is the ancient lodestone of the Sanctuary. And we will remember that the Sanctuary as a whole points north toward the Aegean, while the sign of the initiates was a magnetically charged iron ring marked with a sacred seal. Clearly magnetism was an essential dimension of the Mysteries at Samothrace. But why is magnetism so symbolically important here at the Sanctuary?

There are different symbolic dimensions or levels for understanding the role of magnetism in the Mysteries here. Some of those we have already touched on in our discussion of the sacred geography of the island. For the direction north is associated in Indo-European and especially in Greek tradition with Hyperborea, the mysterious land of the far north to which Apollo traveled, a land of light beyond the duality of day and night. So there is the mythological dimension of sacred geography of the north, which cannot be overlooked.

And there is the stellar dimension of sacred geography, so important for sailors. All who traveled by sea, indeed, all travelers including those on land, were guided by orientation to the Pole Star, which in an earlier era was in the constellation Draco. The symbolism of the Pole orients those who are journeying and who wish to find their way home. Orienting oneself by the Pole star, one can pass through the vicissitudes of sensory and emotional storms, past the Sirens and the clashing rocks, and finally reach refuge. Hence the Mysteries were said to protect travelers.

All this is magnetic, to be sure. But there are other aspects to the mysteries of magnetism as well. Magnetism is invisible, yet is made visible under special conditions. Bring the proper metal, iron, near a magnetic stone and one can see its pull. Likewise, initiation is invisible under most conditions, yet with the right conditions, one can see its effect nonetheless. Furthermore, that effect is invisibly transferable. Hence iron rings can be magnetically charged by magnetite. One can even have a "magnetic chain" that can go from one object to another, just as an initiatic chain goes from initiator to initiate, who becomes an initiator and then in turn has initiates, passed down from time immemorial. Magnetism may be the perfect symbol of initiation in this regard.

We might remark also that magnetism permeates the density of iron—it is an invisible power that penetrates metal. Thus is it perhaps not surprising that the islands of the northern Aegean—Lemnos, Lesbos, and Samothrace—are associated with Hephaestus, god of metallurgy and mining. This makes particular sense given the magnetic rings with the seal of Samothrace, which is to say, rings touched with invisible divine power. And it is perhaps also not surprising that in one myth, Hephaestus, son of Zeus and Hera (king and queen of the gods), has his home on the island Lemnos, where with the nymph Cabeiro, he fathered the Caberoi, in their turn also associated with metalworking. Hephaestus presided over not only metallurgy but also statuary, and in fact had the magical power to animate statues, again, divine power penetrating the densest of materiality.

And then there is Prometheus's iron finger ring. There is, of course, more than one version of the Prometheus myth, but in that of Aeschylus, after Zeus defeated the Titans and decided to kill humans too, Prometheus was concerned for mortals and stole the divine fire from Hephaestus at Lemnos. Subsequently, Prometheus was punished by being chained to a rock and hurled into Tartarus, later chained to Mount Caucasus and torn by an eagle until another immortal agreed to enter Hades for him. Eventually the wounded centaur Chiron [!] agreed to enter Hades on his behalf, and although eventually Prometheus was freed and became an advisor to the gods, he was forced to remember his stealing of the god's fire by having to wear an iron ring. Iron is characteristic of pre-Greek iron age culture; and iron is forged by Hephaestus, given a seal, and made magnetic to remind us of the magnetic divine presence. Prometheus brings the power of the gods to humans and wears an iron ring to remind him/us of that philanthropic mission.

But there is, of course, a corollary anti-magnetism or magnetic repulsion effect, if one might so put it. It was said in antiquity not only that initiation into the Mysteries of Samothrace protected travelers, but also that the island itself was protected from those who were not fated to come to it. Thus the Roman historian Tacitus told the story of Germanicus, heir to the throne under emperor Tiberius, who traveled through the ancient world and sought to go to

Figure 7-1. The sacred stone of Samothrace.

Samothrace. But he was prevented by ill winds from being able to go to the island, and reputedly was told by an oracle of Apollo on the same trip that his death was forecast as imminent, which indeed did happen.[46] The underlying theme seems to be that to even arrive on the island means one is in some sense favored by the protecting deities.

And there is still more. For those who sought initiation were tested, asked what was the worst crime they had committed, thus continuing the theme that the Mysteries promoted virtue and that vice prevented one from being magnetically attuned as an initiate.[47] Thus although all were theoretically allowed to become initiates—male, female, slaves and freemen, nobility and royalty—those who were not virtuous were disallowed. There were also two levels or kinds of initiation, and there were reputedly tests that limited the number of those who entered the higher level of initiation. Again, one could regard initiation as an alignment with a magnetic charge, and vice or lack of virtue as repulsion from that alignment.

At this point, we might also recognize an analogous kind of magnetism—sexual magnetism—that clearly plays a role in the Samothracian Mysteries. But to explore this dimension of the Mysteries, we have to return to some of the mythological themes we touched on earlier, beginning with the theme of the god who is torn apart, and whose genitals are preserved after his death. This mythos is present in ancient Egyptian mythology with the story of Osiris and Isis; it is also part of the mythos of the god Zagreus; it is part of the Dionysian mythos with which Zagreus is associated; and it is part of the mythos of Orpheus, as we saw earlier.

The god Zagreus is one of twin Dionysus gods; Zagreus was said to be the first Dionysus, firstborn son of Zeus and Persephone, whom Zeus had seduced by taking the form of a dragon and then having his way with her. Zagreus was killed by the Titans, who were jealous of him—they cut him into pieces and cooked him in a pot. But Zeus recovered his heart, after which Zeus impregnated Semele, a mortal (said to be the daughter of Cadmus and Harmonia) who in turn bore a second Dionysus, known as Dionysus chthonius. Hence there were twin Dionysus gods, one celestial, one chthonic, just as there were twin Cabeiroi and Dioscuri.

But there is much more to this mythos. For Dionysus Zagreus was said to be the same as the more ancient god Sabazios, and after he was cut apart, his ithyphallic genitals were said to have been recovered by the Cabeiroi of Samothrace and to have been kept upright as the heart of the ancient Mysteries. The relevance of this mythos is corroborated (or commemorated) by the ithyphallic statues at the temple complex and in the harbor. And there is also the story of Demeter at the Mystery site of Eleusis meeting a young woman named Baubo, who famously and pleasingly revealed her vulva to the goddess.[48] The point here is that associated with the Mysteries more generally, both at Samothrace and at Eleusis, was the revelation of the erect penis and the exposed vulva, sexual magnetism expressed in its most essential symbols. Thus it is not surprising that the Mysteries were reputedly associated with orgiastic celebration in secret antinomian rites of Dionysos celebrated at night and associated with the horn or with horns, that is, with oxen, sowing seed, and fertility.[49]

So there is the sexual magnetism celebrated in the Mysteries, a celebration of the source of procreative life itself, but there is also the magnetism of mother and child, celebrated in the *Orphic Hymns* when Demeter is praised as the holy and nurturing mother of fair offspring, the sole daughter with many children. One may recall that the search of Demeter for Persephone is the search of the inconsolable mother for her lost daughter, and that the Eleusinian Mysteries celebrated the divine child, Iakchos (the third Dionysus), and his consort Queen Mise.[50] Dionysus is praised as "two-natured," "two-horned," a "thrice-born" primordial being, and by participating in the Mysteries, we are sharing in the ineffable bond between celestial parent and celestial child. This too is a kind of magnetism.

And there is still another kind of magnetism, which is that of the marriage of the divine couple, symbolized variously by the marriages of gods and goddesses, but in particular by the marriage of Cadmus and Harmonia, associated with Samothrace as well as with Thebes. This marriage, it is said, is especially associated with Samothrace because that was where Cadmus went in search of his abducted sister, Europa. There, it is said, he met Harmonia (daughter of Elektra), and when they married, the gods themselves came bearing gifts. Of course, one of those gifts was the cursed necklace of Harmonia given by Hephaestus. It is said also that Cadmus's companions were killed by a water-dragon at the Ismenian spring, whereupon Cadmus himself killed the dragon. As punishment later in life, Cadmus himself began to grow scales and become a dragon, whereupon Harmonia asked the gods to become serpentine as well, and so the two live as snakes for a time before going to the Islands of the Blessed.[51]

It is worth noting that Kadmilus, among the gods of Samothrace, was associated with Hermes, and that the main symbol of Hermes is the caduceus, a winged staff up which climbs two intertwined (copulating) serpents. The iconography here is actually a hidden form of ithyphallism, for the symbol of Hermes in antiquity was also the *herm,* that is, the erect phallus, sometimes winged. The caduceus encodes this symbolism, and the ithyphallic figures of Hermes and Priapus also were said to protect those journeying at sea, as well as those who might be afflicted by the evil eye. We might note also that a common ancient form of the caduceus shows a staff with two serpents whose heads are at opposite sides, forming what appear to be horns, as well as an opening below (symbolically, the opening of female genitalia). Thus this symbol of Hermes (or Mercury) is associated with the magnetic/ magical power of the staff, the serpent, horns, the phallus, and the vulva.

All of these are, then, subsidiary or contributing aspects of the larger magnetism inherent in initiation into the Mysteries of the Great Gods. That is, the Mysteries invoked or yoked together a host of different kinds of magnetism at once: the actual magnetic orientation toward the north; the magnetic power of the lodestone; the magnetic power of the sacred rings; the magnetic power of the aroused male and female genitals; the magnetic power of the mother searching for the lost daughter; the magnetic power of the parent and the new child; the magnetic power of the marriage of Cadmus and Harmonia; and the magnetic power of the Mysteries as a whole, conveyed to many thousands, yet never revealed to those who are not initiates.

Magnetism is a metaphor that expresses the power of life itself; it is a metaphor for the communicated power of the good, the beautiful and the true. As a metaphor, it expresses the idea of the gods everywhere, found in winds, seasons, starts, animals, fish, plants, below in the underworld, above in the heavens, in the Islands of the Blessed—everywhere. Divine presence is omnipresent and can express itself in human, animal, plant, or other forms, in the elements, anywhere. And one can be attuned to that presence, just as one can be aligned with the attractive field of a magnet.

In this sense one can speak too of magic: magic as practiced in antiquity was understood as aligning one's own purpose with the appropriate form(s) of the divine. Thus in antiquity, one finds all manner of tablets or *defixiones* inscribed with invocations and requests for erotic or other purposes, invoking sometimes a whole string of deities. The idea is that by aligning oneself and one's purpose with the proper deity or deities, through a kind of magnetic response, what one desires will occur. And the objects on which the request is inscribed can be understood, in this sense, as "magnetically charged."

In fact, the entire cosmos can be understood as magnetically charged. All of life is joined together in the great chain or interconnected whole of being, and what joins it can be understood through the metaphor of magnetism. It is not that life can be reduced to magnetism—that isn't the point here. It's rather than one can understand spiritual symbolism as expressing aspects of the divine otherwise not comprehensible to us. This is true of images of lions and eagles, and it is true also of caves and of other initiatory symbols: they are best understood as metaphors conveying something not only visible but also invisible. Indeed, it is true of the island as a symbol too: to it initiates come as if drawn themselves by a kind of magnetism.

Among initiatory symbols, one of the most important is the serpent, often associated itself with magnetic power. Serpents, dragons, in Greek *drakon* (δράκων), with the same root as drakein and derkomai, meaning "to look" or "to see" are as much associated with the mysterious island of Samothrace as is magnetism, for as we will recall, the seal on the magnetic rings of the island depicted two serpents. But what are the meanings of the serpents and dragons that populate ancient folklore, legend, and mythology? And how are serpents and drakontes associated with the Mysteries of Samothrace? To them, and their meanings, we now turn.

Chapter 8
The Dragon

We have seen that magnetic rings of Samothrace featured two serpents, though it is hard to discern whether it is really one serpent with two heads or two serpents intertwined with one another. But it is self-evident that serpents or dragons played an important role in the secret mythology of the island—indeed, a literally central role, since those serpentine images are in the center of the ring insignia. We have already seen that mythology is best understood as a collection of indications concerning different aspects of the divine presence, and that principle is operative here as well. By exploring the mythology of the drakon in antiquity, we can begin to understand at least some of the implications of the serpent(s) signifying Samothracian initiation.

We can begin with the symbolism of the serpent itself, and why it corresponds with initiation. First, we can observe that the serpent emerges from caves or cracks in the earth, that is, symbolically, it moves between the underworld and the world of light. Second, it sheds its skin, that is, it leaves behind its old self and is born anew. Third, it is associated with a class of non-physical, or at least not always visible, serpent-beings that are associated with water both above ground, like lakes and rivers, and below ground, like underground streams and artesian springs. Given the connection we noted earlier between sacred sites and springs and bodies or streams of water, it is hardly surprising that sacred sites are also associated with serpents.

In Greek mythology, we see ambivalence about serpents or *drakontes*. On the one hand, there is a surfeit of heroes whose heroism was demonstrated by overcoming a serpent or dragon. Indeed, Athena herself both fought with serpents and also bore serpent symbolism in her armaments; she both opposed and carried the symbolism of the serpents. And this is true of many heroes and gods, among them Zeus, Pereus, Heracles, and Apollo, as well as Cadmus and Jason—that is, they kill or overcome serpents, but also are in this very act often themselves equivalent to the serpent or drakon, and sometimes later bear those attributes. Cadmus, as we have seen, having killed a *drakon,* at the end of his life (along with his wife Harmonia), even took on the scales and form of one.

But what do we make of this double quality of the drakon as both an extremely dangerous opponent and as symbol of the gods themselves, as indicator of both the infernal and the divine? The drakon is in this regard especially suitable as symbol of the divine, because the divine presence also has the doubled quality of being both exceedingly dangerous and salvific, as potentially terrifically destructive and as the source of healing, as belonging to the underworld, but also to the world of light and air. Thus the symbolisms associated with the drakon include the head of the lion, the wings of a great predator, the body of a great serpent, and fiery or pestilential breath. Not all of these symbols are associated with all myths in antiquity, but nonetheless they form a cluster of characteristics.

The drakon, in some respects at least, symbolizes the divine. The divine presence can be destructive, but also healing; it permeates (moves across) the hierarchy of existence from the hidden underworld to the empyrean. But what of the killing of serpents or dragons? How then to understand that? Does a hero or a god "kill" the divine presence? Not exactly. Rather, the unpredictable wildness of the serpent/drakon is in some respects "tamed" and becomes characteristic of and guardian of a sacred place. Hence Apollo "kills" the great serpent, and yet his priestesses at Delphi are "pythonesses" whose oracular vision is sometimes associated with an underground chamber or source. In brief, the "python" and its "pythonesses," or *pythia*, become symbolically characteristic of Apollo's sacred site Delphi; the serpent-power is become "tamed."

What might the serpent(s) on Samothracian rings signify? For one thing, they invoke all of the symbolism above. Clearly the serpents on the ring face both up and down, meaning that they represent divine power ascending and descending, moving between the worlds. And the serpent is an ambivalent symbol of divine power, because it is at once frightening in a visceral way and yet at the same time fascinating, hence the appellation *drakon* whose root is "to look" or "to stare." Drakontes were known as the "watchers," or guardians of treasure.

But we may also recall that the serpents were consistently associated with the Dioscuri, Castor and Pollux [Polydeuces], who protect travelers and warriors, particularly at sea. The iconography associated with these celestial twins almost always includes serpents. An image on a vase in the British Museum shows the twins on horseback, and even here one sees above them a serpent and a bird of prey (Fig. 8-1). Other images show them having themselves hatched from an egg like serpents, with serpents behind them, or with a column between the twins, a serpent facing each of them.

We saw earlier the importance of the myth of Cadmus and Harmonia, who were directly connected to Samothrace. They were said to have had a daughter, Semele, who in turn was held to be Dionysus's mother in a different version of the myth than the one found in the Orphic Hymns. But in all of the different Dionysus myths, and especially in the Dionysian Mystery traditions, he is associated with wildness, with inebriation or ecstasy, and with various symbolic plants and animals, including the bull, grapes and grape leaves, wine, the panther or tiger, the lion, the dolphin, the bee, but above all, the serpent. Images of maenads in Greek art often show women adorned with serpents, with serpent-head horns above their foreheads (Fig. 8-2).

Now one has to ask why the serpent is linked so closely with the Dionysian tradition. What is the symbolism here? Much as in Hindu and Buddhist forms of Tantra, the Dionysian tradition absorbs the serpent's chthonic power into the divine or, more accurately perhaps, recognizes it too is a divine manifestation. The very thing that is dangerous, fascinating, frightening, that we instinctively avoid and fear, that comes out of the darkness of the earth, the reptilian other, is not ultimately other but reflects hidden dimensions in us.

Dionysianism takes those substances usually forbidden by ascetic religion—inebriating wine, sexual expression, ingestion of meat, wildness—and ritually sacralizes them so that they become not obstacles to spiritual awakening but means. Thus the Dionysian tradition is to regard not so much the organized temple as the primeval wilderness to be sacred, not only the sunny light of day but also the moonlit night, not so much chastity as freedom from inhibition, celebration, the *orgia*, singing, dancing, exhilaration, enthusiasm, from *entheos,* the intoxication and wild freedom of the divine within.

This divine intoxication also may be associated with snake handling, that is, with lack of fear even of venomous serpents or dragons, because again, what before may have seemed to be other, in this state of spiritual ecstasy is known to not be so. The serpent, wildness, sexuality, all of these are not obstacles to but expressions of the divine. Hence to pick up serpents or to be in the wilderness and among the animals is not a step downwards or backwards, as it might seem to us, but rather part of one's experience of transcendence of self and other.

The Dionysian tradition represented by the serpent is primordial; it is the awakening of primordiality in the midst of the iron age, and it is expressed through revelry, music, drumming, dance, celebration, sexuality. It is also magical, hence associated with snake "charming" and with the serpent's and the drakonte's characteristic "looking" or watching, the gaze that is also the power to affect and to effect. One can hardly escape the phallic symbolism of the serpent, either—or the parallel taboos. We alluded earlier to sexual magnetism, and the serpent evokes and symbolizes that power, symbolized by Zeus's seduction of Persephone by taking the form of a snake, the issue of which union, we are reminded, was Dionysus, "Eleutherios," the one who makes free or liberates.

There are larger European connections to the dragon, too, so many that one has to think that there were archaic traditions that have long since been lost except for what traces we can chart. For instance, there is the magical forest of Arthurian legend called Brocéliande in Western France, not far from which is *Le Val sans Retour,* the vale of no return, sometimes held to be an enchanted land in which Morgan le Fay

Figure 8-1. Graphic pen version of 500 B.C.E. image on vase of the Dioscuri with a serpent and a bird of prey.

Figure 8-2. Bas relief of a woman in a Dionysian ecstasy. Note the serpent around her arm and the two serpent "horns" on her head. Note also her wings and the panther, below. Fourth century B.C.E.

held her lovers. Morgan was Arthur's sister or half-sister, and her name, "le Fay," means "of the faeries." Hence it is little surprise that Morgan has some of the same doubleness as Merlin—like him, and for that matter like Viviane, she is sometimes "good" and sometimes "evil." Like these other sorcerers, she doesn't fit a Judeo-Christian moral binary. According to Gerald of Wales, Morgan magically transports Arthur to Avalon and is undoubtedly a revenant of an ancient goddess. In Geoffrey of Monmouth's *Vita Merlini*, when Arthur is wounded, he is brought to the mysterious Isle of Avalon, where Morgan is the chief of nine magical sisters and helps Arthur heal.

And when we look at this entire area not far from Paimpont, France, from above, as from the stars toward Earth, we see something remarkable. *Le Val sans Retour* is situated as a point on the head of a dragon, and in fact, the sacred points of Brocéliande, including the sacred artesian springs of Barenton, and of the Fountain of Youth, when joined by a line, form a shape corresponding to the constellation Draco. And in Draco was the pole star at the time most of the megaliths were raised; in some versions, Draco was much larger than today, encompassing both of the Bears [Ursa Major and Ursa Minor], hence known as *Arctoe et Draco*. Might the name "Arthur" be related to the North [Arktos] and to the Bears, as well as to the Dragon?

What are we to make of the fact that King Arthur's father's name was Uther Pendragon? The word "pendragon" is said to mean "dragon's head," or "chief of the dragons," (*caput draconis*) a name also, incidentally, for the north node of the moon (where the ascending moon crosses the ecliptic), which in turn is linked to eclipses. The south node of the moon is *cauda draconis*, or "tail of the dragon." A solar eclipse occurs when the moon's passage through a node corresponds with the new moon; a lunar eclipse occurs when passage coincides with the full moon. The lunar nodes are on a precessional cycle that lasts 18.59, or close to 19, years, also called the "draconitic cycle."

There is also a dragon association with the greatest collection of standing stones in the world, at Carnac, France, where thousands of stones stand like sentinels arrayed in phalanxes toward the Atlantic Ocean. John Bathurst Deane, a nineteenth-century adventurer and author, referred to the Carnac menhirs seen together as a *dracontium*, meaning that the stones resembled and perhaps were a kind of giant serpent or dragon [*draco*] undulating across the landscape, and indeed the eye, following the stones in their rows, does undulate down one slope and up another in the manner that a great serpent might travel over the land. And John Michell, for his part, thought that standing stones in general were linked to the mysteries associated with dragons in Britain and Brittany, "dragons" in this context referring, he thought, to telluric energies along and above the earth. What then would it mean when, in the Christian era, a man is said to have "killed a dragon"? Might the "killing of dragons" reflect a conflict between imposed monotheism and the more ancient "pagan" [country] traditions represented by these legions of standing stones?

Certainly the *dracontium* of standing stones at Carnac in Brittany represents a tradition far more ancient than any of the monotheisms; and it represents also a testimony to the tradition not in text but in itself as itself. In the stones themselves reside their mysteries, which they are reluctant to disclose. Some Bretons say that the stones are inhabited by dwarves or other beings, each stone its own personality. Indeed the stones are unique, each in some sense like an individual man, and yet they form a collective whose magnitude is miles long, undulating over the landscape toward the Atlantic ocean, called there the Gulf of Morbihan.

In confessional Christianity, the serpent and by extension the dragon are broadly speaking associated largely with evil and to be shunned. In fact, in Christian lexicons of Greek, the word *drakon* is synonymous with "the great Satan." But the archaic pagan tradition concerning dragon and serpent symbolism does not offer such simplistic equivalences. In the ancient traditions, particularly the Greek and Roman ones, it is true that there are serpent and dragon slayers among both gods and human heroes. But it is not the case (as it largely seems to be in Christianity) that the serpent or dragon is simply malevolent and identified with evil. Rather, even when a serpent or dragon is slain in the archaic myths, there often is an equivalence between the dragon and the slayer, and what is more, the serpent or dragon is often subsequently in some respects "tamed" or identified as a protector or as beneficial.[52]

There are stories in antiquity of witches and serpents, like, for instance, the tale in Aristotle's *Mirabilium* in which a Thessalian witch killed a sacred snake (*hieros ophis*) by inscribing a circle on the ground, laying down special herbs, and singing the snake toward her. The serpent also sang as it came, and when it arrived, she could not resist sleeping, for the sacred snake had the power to impose sleep (the same power that the sorceress Medea used when she conquered the snake of Colchis by putting it to sleep through magic). Her son woke her up, she continued to sing, and when the snake entered the circle, it instantly became desiccated.[53] What such a story presents is an equivalence between the sacred serpent and the witch in terms of magical powers, an association that is even more explicit in the tale of Medea and the dragon of Colchis—in at least one version, she weeps and asks forgiveness as she renders him unconscious after having nursed him in earlier times.[54] It is not at all clear that the dragon of Colchis is evil; indeed, he is said to be a "most faithful guardian" of sheep and of the golden fleece.

Of course, there are snake-gods that are beneficial from the outset. Thus, for instance, one finds the form of Zeus called Zeus Meilichios, that is, Zeus as a serpent, often indicated by sacred stones devoted to him.[55] Zeus Meilichios often has a beard and is quite large, significantly larger than a human, while his votive pillars as a whole often resemble a phallus and are sometimes decorated with genitals wherein the penis is replaced by a serpent.[56] Zeus Meilichios is the keeper and dispenser of prosperity and is consistently regarded not as fearful but as kind.

And there is another archaic serpent form that is associated with goodness and prosperity—the Agathos Daimon, literally, the good genius or guiding spirit of prosperity. The Agathodaimon, in Greek tradition, is typically in the form of a serpent and is often associated with the founding of cities or individual habitations as a protector. This is true of Alexandria, founded by Alexander, whose founding myth is that Alexander had a larger serpent in the vicinity killed, after which the serpents of the city, seen as Agathodaimonic, were by order of Alexander himself to be given special offerings of porridge on a festival day.

So closely was the Agathos Daimon associated with the serpent that a man, seeing a snake in the road, might well regard it as a manifestation of the place-daimon, or of his personal or family daimon. The origin of this tradition is undoubtedly primeval in origin, and continued well past antiquity and the advent of the confessional Christianity that tended to regard serpents as the symbolic representation of the devil. Indeed, in antiquity and into Roman times, the visitor to a house might be welcomed as a kind of incarnation of the local Agathos Daimon. The great Roman emperor Julian in fact alluded to this idea, as did Lucian, for the tradition is widespread and ancient.[57]

And there are many associations of the city of Athens with the serpentine place-daimon. We can here allude to just a few. The founder of Athens is said to be Kekrops [Cecrops], an autochthonic king, the lower half of whose body is a coiled serpent. Kekrops is also associated with the founding of the Acropolis as a sacred site. And there still more. According to another myth, Athena visited Hephaestus in search of weapons, but the god was smitten with her and sought to pursue and rape her. She fended him off, but his semen fell on the ground, from which an infant, Erechtheus, was born. Athena put him in a box and gave him to the daughters of Kekrops, telling them not to open the box. Of course they did, however, and seeing therein a serpent-human, this drove them mad and they threw themselves off the Acropolis. Eventually Erechtheus became king of Athens and created the Panathenaic Festival in honor of Athena, his protectress. To him was dedicated the Erechtheion on the north side of the Acropolis, a sacred building home to a sacred snake that was fed by Athena's priestesses. Athenians are known as the "sons of Erechtheus."

From all of these myths and associations, we can see that serpents in general, however fearful some people's reaction to them may be, did not in antiquity have only the kinds of symbolic attributes that we, after millennia of monotheism, are conditioned to see in them. Rather, in antiquity there was a doubleness to serpents and dragons. Heroes kill serpents or dragons associated with water (often springs), but they also can turn into a dragon themselves. One thinks also of the Gigantomachy in which, after the Olympian Gods defeat the Titans, the earth spawns the Giants that seek to defeat the Olympians and restore the Titans, for the Giants of the Gigantomachy had snake legs. Humans who turn into snakes, humans who are part snake, gods who appear in serpent form or are identified with serpents, all of these abound in pagan tradition.

I am not suggesting here that dragons or serpents are not dangerous—it is clear from the ancient traditions that they often are (though not always). And they can also be beneficent, as in the case of Zeus Meilichios or the Agathos Daimon. They can be the guardians of a particular source or body of water, or of a place, or of treasure, and in this capacity may be beneficent, vanquished, tamed, or slain. But often, one could even say almost always, they have a double quality—sometimes they speak in human language, sometimes have human characteristics, sometimes destroy, and sometimes bring bounty.

European folklorists refer to *parédrie*—from *para*, "beside," and *édra*, "seat"—meaning the doubledness of two supernatural beings, or forms of one being, one human and one animal, that serve as guardians. The companion animal may be termed a *paredrus*. Sometimes a dragon or spirit will have a double in another form that is far away.[58] And often it is the case that for human habitation to thrive, the humans must vanquish or at least acknowledge the spirit(s) of a place, which are often in serpent form, serpents/

dragons symbolically joining elements of earth, air, water, and sometimes fire.

What we see, when we look more fully at dragons and serpents in antiquity, is that they must be understood holistically, as part of a constellation of symbols, myths, and attributions. They should be understood in relation to the broader and directly related other archaic European traditions associated with wilderness, mountains, sacred springs, sacred trees, and sacred grottos and caves. To some extent these traditions of sacred landscape were carried on through folklore for centuries, even for millennia, and even under the proscription of Christian authorities. But for sure what happened, with the overlay of confessional Christianity, is a concerted effort at cutting down sacred trees, abandoning the idea of sacred places in the wilderness, and the projection of devil-worship onto those who carried on the ancient folk pagan traditions. This process is very much akin to, even identical with, the projection of "devil" onto serpents and dragons, and their conversion into unambiguously evil beings, as opposed to the multivalences of antiquity.

All this is important as context because Samothrace and the Mysteries belong unambiguously and completely to this archaic understanding of the world, a perspective in which serpents can be symbolic of (or in fact direct manifestations of) the divine, as indeed they are in the seal of the Samothracian ring or in the serpent wrapped around the outstretched arm of the Dionysian maenad. It is this archaic understanding of

Figure 8-3. Kekrops

our human relationship to the natural and spiritual worlds to which Samothrace introduces us. Through it, we see deeper dimensions of the natural world—because we see how nature can in fact manifest and provide portals into the realm of the spirit. We see how humans exist in a world of divine and natural, invisible and visible beings, and engage in exchanges, called sometimes sacrifices or offerings, in order to maintain a larger balance in the cosmos and to prosper.

We shortly will explore further the implications of all these aspects of the ancient Mysteries and archaic ways of understanding humanity, nature, and the divine. But first we need to delve into one more aspect of the Sanctuary of the Great Gods and its Mystery tradition: the Aegean Sea. For as you will recall, the great Sanctuary looks out directly over the sea, whose azure below meets the azure of the sky above. This is the last great key to the Mysteries, the final aspect we will explore before we think more broadly about the Mysteries and their implications for the indigenous archaic traditions of Europe and for us today. But first, we must set out on the wine-dark sea.

Chapter 9
The Wine-dark Sea

From above the ruins of the Hieron at the Sanctuary, looking north past a few trees and some brush, one sees the blue Aegean Sea from the edge of the land out to the horizon. Although we have not discussed it in any detail until now, it is clear that the sea plays an essential role in the Mystery tradition. After all, the Mysteries were long said to encourage initiates to be better, more moral people and to protect sailors on the sea as well as travelers on land. That association with mariners, often linked to the celestial Twins, is undoubtedly the most well-known characteristic of the Samothracian Mysteries. In fact, the Telesterion on the neighboring island of Lemnos—where associated Mysteries (of the Kabeiroi) were celebrated—is on the rocky shore, seeming almost to be upon the sea itself. But what is the spiritual symbolism of the sea?

What are the initiatic meanings of water?

We might begin with the gods and the myths associated with the ocean and with water. Some of them are, of course, obvious, chief among them Poseidon. Even Poseidon contains many enigmatic aspects. And other sea-gods, including goddesses of the sea, are not so well known and often even more enigmatic. To understand them, as always, one has to piece together the different myths, symbols, folk practices, and religious traditions of antiquity in order to develop the larger picture, to understand both more broadly and more deeply what the Mysteries have to do with the sea and the symbolism of the sea.

That there is a connection of Poseidon with Samothrace, and in particular with its highest mountain peak, Fengari, the one who gleams, is clear because that is where he is said to have reclined when watching the Trojan War from afar. We will recall that the name *Samos* is associated with "great height," hence the name "Samothrace," possibly meaning "the island mountain of Thrace." Certainly the island *is* a mountain that rises up from the Aegean, shrouded at the top in clouds and creating its own mysterious microclimate. One can easily see why it might be a legendary perch for a deity. And we could imagine that Poseidon, god of the sea's depths, belongs here.

By some accounts, Poseidon is an archaic god, belonging to an earlier "Pelasgian" or perhaps Indo-European tradition that has to do not only with water or fluidity but also with horses, and it is said that before he was the ocean god, Poseidon was the god of horses and horsemen. Indeed, there are many connections between Poseidon and horses, even in his oceanic persona, where he keeps underwater near his palace teams of water-horses and chariots. With him is associated the *hippocampus*, or sea-horse, which has the head and forelegs of a horse and a serpentine, fish-like tail. Indeed, it is said that Poseidon created the horse in Thessaly, so that the horse is associated with Mount Pelion, the native land of Chiron the centaur, who was tutor of so many mythological figures in Greek tradition.[59]

But what is the meaning of the myriad associations of Poseidon with horses? What have horses to do with the sea? At first, one might think it an incongruous linkage, but on reflection one can see how they are connected, for with the sea is associated travel over the water on ships, while with the earth the comparable form of travel is indeed by horse, either behind a chariot or on its back. In both cases, a human is borne along by wind or like the wind, as the case may be. The ship allows one to travel swiftly over the waters; the horse provides swift travel over land. And in both cases, it is an art to travel successfully.

Poseidon's most noteworthy symbol is his trident, which is often associated with fishing, but which certainly has esoteric significances. The trident is a vertical symbol, corresponding to the world-axis, and it is three-pointed to invoke three realms: the realm above, the realm of the waters, and the underworld. Its three-pointedness also symbolizes the water, the land, and the air, all three of which belong to the god. While he is the master of the waters, he also travels to Olympus and to the human world. He calls forth and subdues storms with his trident; with it he lifts mountains, shakes the earth, and invokes the fertilizing life-force of water.

But another god specifically of the Aegean Sea, toward which the Sanctuary points, is Nereus. Nereus is known as the "old man of the sea" and is often depicted with a human bearded form above, a serpentine finned lower body curled behind him. He is, like Poseidon and so many of the water-gods, a shapeshifter; and indeed, another name for the "old man of the sea" is Proteus, literally, the "first" or "primeval" god, whose very name is synonymous with protean shapeshifting, the ability to take on any form. Proteus is sometimes directly associated with Aegean islands and with Samothrace's sister initiatory island, Lemnos.[60]

In fact, there are direct links between Proteus and the Kabeiric Mysteries of Lemnos, because there were said to be three Kabeiroi that were the offspring of the Nereid Kabeiro, Proteus's daughter, with Hephaestus.[61] Proteus was said to have the power of foretelling the future, and in Homer's *Odyssey*, Menelaus is told by Proteus's daughter how to capture him when he comes out of the ocean. Menelaus indeed captures Proteus, who then turns into a "bearded lion, a snake, a panther, a great boar, then running water, then a towering and leafy tree." But Menelaus holds him fast, so that in the end Proteus ("the lord of secrets") tells Menelaus that the deathless gods

will take him to the Elysian Fields, where the warm
west winds blow, and there are no storms and is no
suffering.[62]

Nereus and Proteus represent the primordial divine
nature that·can take any form, that moves like the
clouds before the wind, that emerges from the waters
and sinks back beneath them, that is the truly archaic
"ground-note" of all the deities. This is particularly
so for he whose life depends on crossing the sea, so
well known for its fickle weather, for tempests and
winds or lack of wind. The wine-dark sea is, of course,
also a metaphor for human life—like Odysseus, we all
seek to cross the waters and reach the "islands of the
blessed," or the Elysian Fields where we no longer
experience suffering. Proteus and Nereus represent
the divine guidance that can bring us to that enduring
home.

But there are sea-goddesses as well, and they too
play a part in the Mysteries' symbolism. They are
celebrated in the *Orphic Hymns*, where we read
that in the train of Nereus (the shaker of Demeter's
earth) and his wife Doris are the fifty beautiful and
irreproachably ethical Nereides, their daughters.[63]
Among them are Thetis and Amphitrite, goddesses
of the sea, protectors of sailors, and riders on or
with dolphins. The Nereides belong to the Aegean as
the Naiads belong to freshwater, and the Oceanides
belong to the great Oceans. Each of the Nereides has
her particular association, one with caves, another
with calm seas, another with swift and beneficial
winds. They are often depicted nude, or as mermaids,

as beautiful, and as beneficial to humans. One of them is Kabeiro, mother of the divine twins of the Kabeiroi.

And there are associations between many of these immortals and Dionysus. One of the early tales of Dionysus concerns his being driven from the land by a hostile king, Lycurgus, and taking refuge in the Aegean with Nereus's daughter Thetis. Thetis, it is said, sheltered Dionysus under the sea. Later, Dionysus returned to the land, revealing himself as a god and drawing crowds of ecstatic women into his train. (Pausanius remarked that they were women from the islands of the Aegean.)[64] Ovid refers to Dionysus as "conqueror of India," underscoring the connection between Dionysus and Shiva, who as we've seen, share many characteristics in common.[65] Finally, it is said that Dionysus descended into the underworld to rescue his mother, Semele, and that the "nocturnal rites" of Dionysus, which Pausanius observes cannot be spoken of in detail, celebrate this recovery and what is sometimes described as his "sharing immortality" with her.[66] Dionysus was known in Roman sources as "Father Liber" or "Liber," meaning "the one who liberates." When Hephaestus trapped Hera in a golden chair, it was Dionysus who got Hephaestus drunk and transported him to Olympus so as to free Hera, which he alone could do.

What are we to make of all these associations? As so often with the ancient gods, one finds such an intricate net of symbols and names and associations that it is hard to discern the larger meanings. Yet as always, those meanings are there if one steps back a bit. Above all, we might observe that all of these immortals are protean. They typically have human form, or at least are so depicted, but they transform, effortlessly move between realms, share characteristics of different realms. With them, human and serpent and fish are combined. Dionysus is not a sea god, but there he is in the bed of the Aegean with Thetis; he is human, but he ascends to Olympus, after revealing himself to be a god; he engages in war and is seen in the city, but belongs also to the mountains and wild places. So too Zeus, and Poseidon, and especially Nereus and Proteus change form easily—none of them can be "fixed." All are fluid.

In the technocratic world, one does not think of water itself as divine, or as home to divinities or water spirits—the very idea seems foreign. But that foreignness is because we of European heritage have long since forgotten our indigenous traditions, which were assiduously stamped out by the incursion of confessional Christianity over the past two millennia. Many of the Christian saints as well as the synods proscribed traditional recognition of sacred places in the wilderness and, most especially, the sacredness of artesian springs, rivers, lakes, and seas. Further, confessional Christianity denounced the immortals of those places and waters as "demons" or "devils" or the like.

Yet telltale hints of the ancient ways still remain, even today. Who has not seen a fountain into which people have tossed pennies or other forms of coinage? That is actually a sacrifice, a gift to the spirit of the water in that place—or at least, this is the tradition it echoes. And there are many indigenous sacred places in Europe to this very day, recognized as such by the local people. I have been to a sacred spring that flows deep within a forest. The local people still go on pilgrimages there and anoint themselves with the pure water that flows from the earth; and the sacredness of the place is so strong that it radiates almost tangibly. It is protected to this day by its own inner power. Such a place is home, the ancients said, to a numinous being, and that being is the protean manifestation of the living power of the place.

Indeed, bodies or sources of water, the ancient Europeans believed, were inherently sacred places, and there was a festival day to recognize and honor them, the Neptunalia, celebrated traditionally on July 23. The Neptunalia (named, of course, for the Latin name of Poseidon, Neptune) was sacred for sailors and fishermen, of course, but it extended also to inland waters and to springs—to all sacred water. Lucan gives a striking description of a sacred grove in France that Caesar had ordered destroyed, featuring sacred trees of great antiquity and deep, cold springs.[67] By the seventh, eighth, and ninth centuries, Neptunalia was explicitly proscribed by Christian officials, but so was "casting bread and wine into springs" or any kind of gifts or sacrifices to the immortals or spirits of the waters, stones, trees, wilderness grottos, wells, rivers, lakes, and so forth.[68]

What were the indigenous people of Europe seeking with such practices of recognizing the water beings, spirits, or god, goddesses, Nereides, Naiads, and the like? As it turns out, much the same aims were sought as were characteristic of the Mysteries of Samothrace, in particular, protection, prosperity, fertility, and morality. Water is essential to life, as is the stability of the cycles of water, that springs continue to flow, that rains fall upon crops, that storms do not destroy, that ships be brought by safe breezes to their destinations. The indigenous belief was that the cycles of our physical world depend upon invisible or rarely visible beings and our relationship to them, and especially to sources of water. For the ancients, the visible sacred place is portal to the invisible.

There are two aspects of water that are both important for understanding some of the roles of water in or at sacred sites. The first is, relevant to the ancient Greek mythological traditions we have been looking at, is that water itself is protean and can take all manner of forms—sea-waves, sea-foam on the shore, placid cerulean waters, violent high waves, mist, clouds, fog, rain, ice, snow. And the second is related to this—that water, whatever form it takes, is fundamentally still water, thus representing the ideal metaphor for the underlying unity of the many forms of the divine.

Hence water at sacred sites so often symbolizes purity or purification. To dip into the water, to be immersed in it, to sprinkle water, all symbolize cleaning away one's accumulated dirt, both literal of course and metaphorical. And this purification is in essence a return to the pristine unity of the human being and nature in primordiality, what Mircea Eliade referred to as *ab origine*, that is, in the very beginning, when timelessness is experienced in time, hieratically. The *Telesterion* at Lemnos, on the edge of the island, and the sanctuary of Samothrace that looks out over the Aegean evoke the primordial human on the primordial sacred island arisen in the great blue water.

One of the secret names of the Samothracian initiates was said to be the Saoi, "those who belonged to Mount Saos," but also "those who are rescued from danger" (in particular, from danger on sea voyages).[69] The initiates were said to be under the protection of the female deity, Elektra, another of whose names was said to be Strategis.[70] Is there a deeply archaic pattern of the warrior band under the aegis of a female deity who has many names and aspects and who protects the band during its voyages, adventures, and occasional plundering?

Samothrace, as an island mountain rising up from the Aegean, was itself symbol of the sacred and portal to the invisible in the midst of the sea. Another ancient name for Samothrace was Melité, the same root as the island name "Malta," with the connotation of honey and bees, an indication of the island's fertility, and indeed even today it is home to olive groves and meadows of wildflowers.[71] The sea is a constant presence on the island—one is always aware that earth exists in relation to the water, not, as inland, seemingly on its own.

The three islands associated with the Mysteries

together were Samothrace, Lemnos, and Imbros, and of their connected Mysteries Strabo wrote that although the myths and the names are dizzying in their variety and apparently confusing, what underlies them is not so difficult to understand.[72] It is common, he continued, that the Greeks and their archaic predecessors performed their sacred rites often accompanied by music and dance, in particular percussion instruments that encouraged ecstatic, rhythmic movement. Music and dance draw the mind away from ordinary worries or pursuits and orient it toward the divine and timeless. Hence the connections also between art with prophecy, because a foreteller of the future, like an artist, draws from timelessness or eternity. Religious rites accompanied by music and dance bring practitioners out of themselves and put them in touch with eternity beyond the realm of the senses.[73]

We moderns look at the dizzying array of deities, names, and myths associated with the Mysteries and we want to come up with one set of deities or myths that explain everything. But that's not how it works. Rather, we might be wiser to think of the different deities and myths as fluid and protean, all different manifestations of the underlying divine reality in which one experiences what is true, beautiful, and good. The different heroes and demi-gods, like Jason or Herakles, were initiated into the Mysteries because that put them in touch with the divinities; they demonstrate that there is continuity between the human and divine worlds, fluidity between them.

When initiates, particularly in the Dionysian or Bacchic traditions, went into religious frenzy, they were going beyond the human, beyond the world of duality and social stricture, outside the bounds of propriety. This is why the Dionysian Mysteries were connected to wild places, to mountains and wilderness—they brought into the human world transcendent and unjudgeable power like a lightning bolt from a storm. This is also the symbolism of the wine associated with Dionysus and with the island Mysteries, for wine, music, dance, and sexual license all conduce to the transcendence of the self, transcendence of social mores. This is why the Mysteries were open to all: because in initiatory transcendence there is neither slave nor free, neither man nor woman.

The symbol of the dolphin cutting ecstatically through the waves, leaping above the water and rushing through it, expresses this state of divine unity that we are referring to here. The Mysteries were clearly, ultimately, about celebration, and were to be celebrated, because they brought initiates into the protean state of being above and prior to the world of the senses, prior to social strictures. The dolphin celebrates life by its very being in the water, hence it is an ideal symbol of the divine, and especially of the deities of the sea.

The Korybantes (the warriors who danced with swords) and the Maenad women in the Dionysian train of dancers and celebrants represent this fusion of the human and the divine through motion like that of the dolphin in the sea. I remember well, as our ship approached Samothrace from the mainland, watching the dolphins leap over the spreading of its white wake. That play, the joyous unity with the water, is very much akin to the divine unity of the dances both male and female that expressed and celebrated the Mysteries.

And beyond all these aspects of the Mysteries is something else that we cannot forget about the island. On it, it is as if we are ourselves the first humans, primordial man and woman on the green mountain of land rising up in the midst of the sea.[74] In and on such a place, we are primordial humanity on the island of the blessed, where the gods are not far at all, and we can through our journeys and adventures also deepen and heighten our own realization of the divine. For the deities of the sea tell us above all that protean deity expresses itself everywhere, in the trees, in the hot springs and waterfalls, in the slow clear pools of water, in the sea, in the rocky shore, on the heights of the mountain, in the meadows and among the olive trees, in the misty clouds on the island's peak. Deity, the sea gods show us, can express itself everywhere and through any one.

And there is a grand metaphor for this unity expressed as union of a man and a woman: the hieros gamos, the last and most intimate aspect of the Mysteries. To it we now turn.

Chapter 10
Hieros Gamos

The Greek term *hieros gamos* (ἱερὸς γάμος) refers to "sacred marriage" and can be understood in a variety of ways. Strictly understood, the term "sacred marriage" can be understood as a wedding of two divinities, an example of which would be the marriage of Zeus and Hera. However, the term has not always been interpreted in this strict way, and indeed, to understand the term symbolically or in contemporary usages, other definitions of *hieros gamos* are necessary. The *hieros gamos* is associated with fertility cults, the idea being that human ritual invokes spirits or gods in order to promote human and agricultural fertility. As we will see, though, the ancient *hieros gamos* is not quite what many might think it is.

Although the argument for a strict-sense interpretation of *hieros gamos* (as referring only to the marriage of two deities) is persuasive on its own terms, the term is used much more broadly to refer to "sacred marriage" understood symbolically. Hence *hieros gamos* also could be applied to more one-sided cases of symbolic marriage, for instance, the Roman Vestal Virgins. The Vestal Virgins were pledged to remain unsullied by sexual intercourse on pain of death, a tradition that had them in effect "married" to Rome itself, Rome not as a secular city but as a divine or transcendent male warrior archetype. Such a use still does convey to some degree the notion of *hieros gamos*, just as (evidently) did some of the initiatic Mysteries. Whether between gods, between gods and humans, or between humans invested with divine symbolism, as long as sexually polarized male/female participation in the divine is part of the religious construct or ritual, the notion of *hieros gamos*, however far afield it may seem, still may be applicable.

The most famous example of the *hieros gamos* is the marriage of Zeus and Hera, which is, of course, a sacred union in the strictest sense, that is, the wedding of a god and a goddess, said to have taken place variously on the island of Samos, or the island of Crete, or in the Garden of the Hesperides. One might think that the wedding of the god and goddess would be a happy affair in which humans could participate vicariously, but their sacred marriage, like that of Cadmus and Harmonia, seems to have been unfortunate in many respects. In fact, the goddess Hera herself is a remarkably conflicted figure, as is Zeus.

One is challenged to elaborate all the peculiar

aspects of this archetypal wedding of the gods, but here are a few of them. First, Zeus and Hera are actually brother and sister, both being the offspring of Kronos. Then, Zeus seduces Hera by subterfuge, pretending to be a bedraggled cuckoo that she takes pity on and holds to her breast, upon which the god reveals himself and embraces her. Third, Hera then bedazzles Zeus with a garment borrowed from Aphrodite, so their relationship more or less symbolizes mutual inveigling. And both Zeus and Hera are notorious for their jealousy and temper tantrums, not to mention Zeus's seductions of countless goddesses and mortals. Finally, the "happy couple," patron and patroness of marriage, have as issue the god Ares, god of war, whom Zeus detests. And Hera gives birth to the crippled dwarf god Hephaestus through parthenogenesis, as well as to Typhon, the monster that was to overthrow Zeus.

What's more, these are only initial indicators of how the supposedly paradigmatic *hieros gamos* was not necessarily a strictly paradisal union. After all, Hera was renowned for her maliciousness—she mercilessly stalked the hero Herakles and sought to have Dionysus thrown into the sea. Hera sought to kill Hephaestus by herself throwing him into the sea, after which, as we will recall, he trapped her in a manacle-equipped chair or throne from which only Dionysus was able to convince him to release her. In fact, one is compelled to wonder what sort of divine model Hera is.

Then there are the festivals of Hera. These too

are a bit strange. Walter Burkert summarizes the *Heraia* as fundamentally a rupture in the divine order, with Zeus and Hera angry with one another, Zeus threatening to go off with another woman and retiring far away. Zeus then has a wooden doll dressed up as a competing bride and conveyed in an ox-pulled cart to the festival—upon which an angry Hera rushes to the festival and rips away her rival's clothing, revealing the truth for all. The divine couple then reunite, and the rival along with sacrifical bull and cow are all burnt in a great pyre, so divine order is restored in the end.[75]

Another prototypical sacred wedding was that of Cadmus and Harmonia. Cadmus was a hero, born the son of a king and queen in Phoenicia, whose sister, Europa, had been abducted by Zeus when he was a young man. His father commanded him to go forth and rescue his sister, and he, his mother, and his "brother" Thasos traveled to Samothrace, there becoming initiates. It was there, also, that Cadmus met Harmonia. There are different accounts of Harmonia: in one, she was the daughter of Zeus and Elektra, her brothers then being Dardanos and Iason, founding figures of the Mysteries; while in another, Harmonia was the daughter of Ares and Aphrodite, the god of war and the goddess of love. She was the patroness of harmony in love and war, whose opposite was Eris, goddess of strife.

Cadmus and Harmonia were married in a wedding to which the gods were invited and came bearing gifts, and the Muses sang captivating wedding songs.

Demeter brought the couple corn; Hermes brought a lyre; Athena brought a necklace, a robe, and a flute; Elektra gave them the rites of the great mother, accompanied by cymbals and kettledrums.[76] Thus the wedding of Cadmus and Harmonia might seem to have been most auspicious, and indeed, afterward, the two of them did bear among their children Ino, the sea nymph, and "white-armed fair Semele," who coupled with Zeus himself.

But the necklace given to Harmonia at the wedding had been crafted by Hephaestus and brought misfortune to the couple. Cadmus did found the city of Thebes, which was linked with Samothrace in its Mysteries, and its acropolis became known as the *Cadmeia*. But he also killed the dragon at the Ismenian spring, which then caused Ares, the god of war, to require penance from him. The adventuring Cadmus and Harmonia became king and queen of various cities as well as the kingdom of Illyria, and they had illustrious children and grandchildren, but they also suffered, in the end both turning into serpents before finally being translated to the islands of the blessed.

And there is still another famous *hieros gamos* that continues the same theme, the marriage of Peleus and Thetis. Peleus was a mortal hero, while Thetis was a Nereid daughter of Nereus and Doris. Thetis had been raised by Hera, and when Hephaestus was thrown from Olympus to the island Lemnos, it was Thetis who cared for him. Initially, Zeus and Poseidon wanted to be with Thetis, but having heard a prophecy that her son would become ruler of the gods, they determined it best for her to marry a human. Peleus captured Thetis, on the advice of the centaur Chiron, by binding her with ropes. She changed rapidly (in the manner of her father Nereus) into fire, water, wind, a tree, a bird, a lioness, and a serpent, but finally returned to her female goddess-form and agreed to marry Peleus.

The wedding of Thetis and Peleus was said to have taken place on Mount Pelion, home of the centaur Chiron, and among their wedding gifts were the immortal horses Balius and Xanthus, which later were the steeds of their warrior-son, Achilles. The gods and goddesses were invited to the wedding, except for Eris, goddess of discord, who in retaliation gave a golden apple inscribed "to the fairest," which Athena, Aphrodite, and Hera all interpreted as referring to them. The dispute was resolved by Paris, who chose Aphrodite, who in turn promised Paris the beautiful Helen of Troy, and thus brought about the Trojan War.

The guiding theme, in other words, of the *hieros gamos* is clearly not that a marriage of or to the gods is full of peace and delight only. Of course, this is perhaps contrary to modern interpretations in which the idea seems to be that through ritual a human couple can channel and unite as god and goddess. For in all of these signature examples of the *hieros gamos*, the marriage of the gods or the wedding attended by the gods is actually the occasion for trials. Even the marriage of Hera to Zeus, Hera being the goddess of marriage, produces as offspring the god of war, Ares, the crippled dwarf god Hephaestus, and the sea monster Typhon.

But the *hieros gamos* in fact has a very different purpose than what we moderns might attribute to it. The *hieros gamos* represents what we could term a vicarious set of trials that the god and goddess or hero and heroine undergo in order that we mortals do not have to. There is a tragic dimension to the *hieros gamos*, or alternatively put, a series of misfortunes attributed to a wedding gift (the necklace given to Harmonia, the golden apple given by Eris, and so forth) that produces trials for the representative couple in place of those that humans might undergo. In this sense the function of the divine wedding is to depict and draw away discord from the human world by depicting and resolving it in the myth.

And there is an esoteric way of understanding these different myths of divine marriages. Seen esoterically, they are best understood—as indeed is much of Greek mythology—in an initiatory context. Now initiation is not only sweetness and light—typically, initiation consists rather in catharsis. The initiate experiences in the initiatic ritual darkness and fear, loss and even terror, in order to come out the other side and experience light and joy. These various myths of *hieros gamos* are actually initiatory tales—as is particularly obvious in the *Heraion* ritual wherein the quarrel between Zeus and Hera is depicted and then resolved.

The origin of what we understand today as theater is actually in the Mysteries. The initiation itself undoubtedly was theatrical in that initiation was dramatic: initiates would experience the loss of Persephone and her recovery; they would experience the descent into the underworld; and they would experience the light and joy of the telestic conclusion, which was also *telein,* that is, fulfillment. But an important part of the Sanctuary at Samothrace also was the theater located on the western hill across the sacred stream from the initiatory buildings, the seats made of white limestone and reddish porphyry.

The theater provided theatrical accompaniment and support for the Mysteries, conveyed not so strictly as in ritual, but more in what we might call a para-initiatory form. The same is true of the various festivals, with pageants and other events that brought the Mysteries outside the precincts of the Mysteries proper—these too are para-initiatory. What we think of now as theater is a secularized form of what originally was an accompaniment to and support for the drama of the Mysteries. For theater to become resacralized would require first a recovery of the Mystery tradition itself—theater would have to return to the source, an idea we will explore later.

The ancient *hieros gamos,* whether by that one refers to the mythical marriage or the festivals, pageants, and dramas that depicted it, represents also the permeability of divine and human realms. The irascibility of Zeus, the vengefulness and spite of Hera, their impetuousness, all these are most clearly human qualities. Likewise, Cadmus and Harmonia (and Peleus, for that matter) are human, yet the gods attend their wedding, bringing gifts, no less. In antiquity the gods and humans crossed over easily into one another's worlds; and what is more, one might (like Peleus) marry an immortal, or like Cadmus become immortal, or a woman might be impregnated by Zeus. What all of this means is that the *gamos,* the union, is always an hieratic occasion, that is, it reveals divinity in the human realm and humanity in the divine realm.

And there is a hidden link between every one of these hieratic weddings—the lame dwarf Hephaestus. Hephaestus is, we will recall, putatively the offspring of Zeus and Hera, except that he was born parthenogenetically from Hera, who then flung him from Olympus to Lemnos. Lemnos then became the smith's home base, as it were, and he was cared for by Thetis, the very sea nymph who later married Peleus. And it was Hephaestus who forged the unfortunate necklace that was later given to Harmonia at her wedding. What are we to make of this link between Hephaestus and each of these instances of *hieros gamos*?

The answer has to do, actually, with the era in which we find ourselves still today, the iron age. We will recall that there were said by the Greeks (reflecting a much older tradition) to be four ages: gold, silver, bronze, and iron. Ours is the iron age, and as it turns out, Hephaestus is the god who works iron, is associated with mining, forges, machines, technical ingenuity.

It was Hephaestus who fashioned an intricate chair device to trap Hera; his ingenuity produced not only weapons but all sorts of innovations, from jewelry to machinery. And it was from Hephaestus that Prometheus stole the god's fire to give it to humanity, thus making possible for humans what Hephaestus did for the gods.

In earlier times, there were Titans, and giants as well as heroes among men, but it is Hephaestus who signals the modern iron age, and that is an era of symbolically lame dwarves, that is, of an era of decline. In the earlier age, the divine wedding might have been a golden affair, full only of delight, but in the iron age, the gold is only in the golden apple of discord; the conflict between men and women is visible among the gods and goddesses too. The presence of Hephaestus in all these celebrated weddings of antiquity signals to us that they belong to the iron age. The wedding of Cadmus and Harmonia may not have been the first attended by the gods, but it may well have been the last. It took place at the end of the earlier age and the beginning of our own, yet partook in the magic of those earlier eras in which it was not so unusual for the gods to walk among humans.

Here too, there is a parallel with the Indian tradition, and especially with Tantra. In Tantra, too, ours is said to be an era of decline and discord, an iron age termed the Kali Yuga. And the gods and goddesses of Tantra, Shiva and Kali, for instance, represent even more "negative" qualities than Zeus and Hera. If one thinks Hera is frightful with her vengefulness, then consider

Kali with her necklace of skulls and other alarming attributes! There are many parallels, as we have seen, between Shiva and Dionysus, not the least of which is that both are gods of wine and eros, and both belong to the iron age of decline, where such approaches to the divine may indeed be more appropriate.

In such an iron age, it is important that we humans be able to recognize ourselves in our divinities, that they reach us where we are. What is more, divinities like these are transformative—that is, they include a host of symbols that outwardly appear to be disturbing or even terror-inducing, like the necklaces of human skulls, or capes made of human skin, or skull-cups filled with blood or nectar, but that inwardly symbolize the transformation of these "negative" into "positive" qualities. Hekate represents such a divinity—she represented night and the creatures of night and nightmare—and thus also healing and renewal, because by embracing such a divinity and recognizing her as divine, one is able to also transmute one's own "dark side" into liberation. In the Mysteries, not only night, and nightmarish phantasms, but also sexuality, wine, dance, music, and food all may be incorporated into and transformed by the religious path.

And the *hieros gamos* also reflects this inclusive transmutation of what might be construed as "negative" into a part of the religious path. We have been given hints that the myth of Cadmus and Harmonia was incorporated into the initiatic mythology of Samothrace, wherein Harmonia was a form of Persephone, rescued by Cadmus, the rescue resulting in their reunion and their sexual union, hence the ithyphallic images. Whereas a moralistic religious tradition like confessional Christianity deplored and detested sexually explicit references or images, and the Church Fathers were unremitting in their denunciations, the Mysteries, which were also held to be a morally uplifting tradition, took an entirely different path, one not of renunciation but transmutation.

The nude male with an erect phallus reveals the unapologetic embrace of life, the return to a primordial state marked by the absence of shame, in which vitality and beauty are part of the religious path itself. The Mysteries at Samothrace and on the other islands conveyed into historical times archaic, indeed, primordial ways of being in the world, hence the associations between the Mysteries of the islands and the Titans, the elder gods. The *hieros gamos* includes not only positive but also negative symbolism, and all is incorporated into a larger dramatic, cathartic whole that ultimately represents the re-emergence of primordial humanity *ab origine*, that is, belonging not to time but to timelessness and also to the first time, that is, to the revelation of timelessness, light, and the invisible magnetic power of life itself as manifested in ritual at these remarkable sacred sites.

The Mysteries culminated in the revelation of light in the night, followed by ecstatic dance and music, celebration, and a great feast with wine and meat. The secret *hieros gamos* or divine wedding is that between the different aspects of ourselves, between us and the gods, between us and one another, in short, the restoration of our own individual and collective wholeness because, as members of the confraternity of initiates, we are brought into the soterio-community of those who will after death experience the "two lights," that is, the two-in-one unity that is also represented symbolically by the "islands of the blessed" and by the Western islands, the garden-islands that belong not to time but to eternity. The symbolism of marriage is the symbolism of union and also of re-union; it is restoration to primordial wholeness. This is why it culminated the Mysteries.

Ultimately, the Mysteries point us—in our modern conditions of diaspora and loss of connection to our own traditions—toward restoration of our own individual and collective wholeness. They remind us very clearly of indigenous Europe, that there *is* an indigenous Europe, that behind and beyond the overlay of imported monotheisms, there were much more ancient and deeply rooted indigenous European traditions. The Mysteries, for all their enigmatic aspects, for all their fluidity and ungraspability, are ultimately a reminder not only of who we once were but also of who we can be. Because they continually emerge into time from timelessness, they cannot disappear. And in our next chapter, we will explore what their continual presence means for us today.

Chapter 11
The Ancient Greeks and the Present Age

In the fragments we have of his work "Purifications," Empedocles describes the transmutation of a mortal (perhaps himself) into a god, who is recognized as such by other people, is crowned as a god and festooned with sacred ribbons and flowering wreaths, gathers followers and celebrants, and receives requests for wealth, for prophecies, for cures, for freedom from long suffering.[77] He explains that because of the shedding of blood in ages past, his daimon had to reincarnate among fishes and birds, and among men, separated from the blessed lands for thirty thousand years, until finally he became a philosopher, a physician, a healer, a prophet, and a god. There are here—in the work of Empedocles and his predecessor

Parmenides, and in the works of others among the ancients—keys to the secrets of the Mysteries of the Great Gods that make them at least a little more comprehensible, even in our present day.

But we should begin with what must be termed the "Greek miracle."[78] And that is the magnificence of what the ancient Greeks achieved, to begin to appreciate which one must stand where the ancient Greeks stood on the Acropolis, gazing upon the beauty of ancient temples with their perfect pillars, their perfect statues. The sublimity of ancient Greek art and architecture, of its mythological and literary and philosophical and political richness, has no equal in the world. How is it that all of this came to be in this warm, dry, and rocky land? What accounts for all these astonishing achievements, which cannot be appreciated let alone begin to be understood unless one is actually there, among them?

An iconic image in the Louvre, the wingéd goddess Nike, once stood like so many other extraordinary and sublime masterpieces of statuary and ancient art at the Mystery complex at Samothrace. The fineness, the subtlety of these images crafted of ancient marble, the otherworldly beauty and perfection of the temples of the gods, the initiatory buildings celebrating the ancient Mysteries, what can account for them? In the Acropolis museum, in other great museums of Greece, and as plunder in other museums of the world, stand nonpareil images, so captivating in their perfection that one has no words to describe them. Each of these images is itself like a god in human form.

And there is a key. For the Greek miracle *is* a revelation; it results from exactly what Empedocles shared in his poetic fragments on "purification," that the different realms of being are not separate but flow into one another, that we can move between human and animal realms, but also between the world of man and the realm of the gods. What we see, when we gaze upon these most superb works of art is indeed divine. And that is one of the secrets of the ancients vital for us today to begin to comprehend. Empedocles had it exactly right: the Greek miracle was nothing less than the manifestation of the divine in the human world. This is what culture—and the Greek miracle is culture at its purest—really is.

I write "divine," here, not "the Divine," because the article *the* objectifies what, in the Greek miracle, is at once dynamic and static, frozen movement, marble that expresses Elysium. Elysium is, of course, a secret meaning of the other most famous Mysteries, those of Eleusis. It is a common mistake to believe that the ancient Greeks or, for that matter, the ancient Europeans saw the gods as each entirely discrete and objectified, as though polytheism had no center. What we see at Samothrace, what we experience there, is that the gods had many names and, what is more, that beyond the many gods is their divine nature or, to put it another way, the many gods all manifest divinity. The gods are not fixed but dynamic, and the barrier between us and them is permeable.

What Empedocles shows us is that we and the gods share a continuum, just as we and nature share a continuum. Modern science recognizes some of the relationships between man and animal, for instance, but we do not seem to have language for expressing the upper register of that continuity, the range from humanity to the gods. This is what ancient indigenous Europe has to offer us; it is what we need to hear. But it offers itself to us only indirectly, only through clues and through places, through the ancient stone monuments of great antiquity, through the hints of myths, and through the fragments divulged by philosophers and historians.

Those who feel called back to their indigenous European roots need to recognize that those roots go far deeper even than a primeval sacred sanctuary made of archaic stones. In this, too, Samothrace offers us guidance. For the island as a whole is sacred, and has other, even more archaic sacred sites on it. We have already seen that the mountain is sacred. On a hill near the town of Choros are dolmens, archaic great stone slabs with an orientation that opens to the west-northwest, that is, toward a combination of the direction north, the symbolism of which we explored earlier, and west, the direction of the blessed islands. Both directions are associated with paradisal lands where time does not hold sway as it does on earth.

Dolmens are sometimes also graves, where a hero or heroes are interred, sacred sites often (as on Samothrace) with an artesian spring nearby, but also with a view of the sea. These are sacred places that mark the juncture of this-worldly life and a heroic or divine afterlife, the movement out from the chthonic darkness between the great stones near running water to the light and the sky above the sea. These archaic monuments were said in local folklore to have been built by cyclopes or giants, or perhaps by the titans and elder gods. But they belong to a time even more archaic than that of the Mysteries.

And older still is the sacred cave of Hekate on the other side of the island. The ancient accounts are not entirely clear, but Lycophron refers to "Zerynthos, the cave of the goddess [on Samothrace] to whom dogs are slain,"[79] and refers to her as "Brimo Trimorphos," or "three-formed [three-faced] Angry and Terrible One."[80] And Strabo remarked that the Korybantes and the Kouretes were regarded in his day as the male and female celebrants of the goddess Hekate, observing that Dionysus, Hekate, the Muses, and Demeter all are associated with sacred branches or wreaths, choral dances, music, and initiations (as indeed characterized the Mysteries at the Sanctuary).[81] Even Nonnus, on whom one cannot place too much weight, refers to Samothrace's cave of "Zerynthos of the unresting Korybantes, the home of renowned Perseis (the Destroyer) [Hekate], where the rocks are thronged with torchbearing initiates of the goddess."[82]

Hekate represents an extremely ancient archetype, today often considered to be that of the goddess of the underworld and the night, the leader of a pack of dogs, but in antiquity a bearer of light in the darkness, carrier of a torch (*phosphoros*), the chthonic one (Χθονιη), who bears three faces, and whose face can be frightening and fiery (Brimo: Βριμω), an epithet also sometimes applied to other goddesses, whose names might include Bendis, Persephone, Demeter, Cybele, Rhea, and Artemis. Again, we must approach the goddesses not as entirely discrete individuals but as different names and aspects of an underlying force that has its own reality and associations, but which we humans see and interpret.

Here, finally, we begin to see additional, even more archaic aspects of the ancient island's mythological clues begin to take shape, rising up out of the mist of history. For Hekate does not represent only chthonic mysteries. When we turn to ancient texts, we find that Hekate is a very different figure than the way she is often depicted in the later period or indeed in many contemporary depictions. What are some of Hekate's characteristics that pertain to Samothrace? We will recall the myth in which Persephone was abducted into the underworld and Demeter sought her return. Demeter's guide in the underworld was Hekate, hence Hekate has the role of psychopomp, or guide through the realms of the spirit.

Hekate was the only of the titans, the pre-Olympian gods, who was allowed by Zeus to continue into the new order, and further, she was given authority over (if one may so put it) the sky, the earth, and the underworld.[83] Her association with crossroads and doorways (her image was often put outside doorways in ancient Greece) and her mythical role as psychopomp all make it clear that she was, like Hermes, one who could pass from one realm to another, and who further had the keys or the passes to allow her to let others pass through. She is unique among the ancient deities in that she is associated not only with the underworld but with the cosmos (above, on earth, and below), much like Sophia in the later Christian mystical tradition. She is the guide of souls, but identified also with the soul of the cosmos as a whole, and with the ensoulment (birth) as well as the posthumous destiny of humans (the afterlife).

Hekate is also unusual because she is often depicted in statuary as having triplicate form, that is, as three different back-to-back female forms, facing out in three directions. She is sometimes depicted as having animal heads, in which case the respective animals are sometimes said to be a horse, a dog, and a lion, though she is frequently identified with the dog and the pole-cat.[84] She is often depicted with two torches, the two lights reminding us of those on the Samothracian seal-rings. Hekate sometimes is associated with other symbols, including keys and a serpent, and sometimes also is associated, like Janus, with two faces to emphasize her moving both ways between realms.

Because of her unique characteristics, Hekate had a major role in the theurgic tradition of late Platonism, not least because of the role she played in that mysterious text of antiquity, *The Chaldean Oracles*. *The Chaldean Oracles* include a number of references to Hekate, for instance, a fragment in which Hekate herself says that

From limitless dawn filled with stars,
I leave the pure, vast divine home,
and come to the nourishing earth,
following the call of your ineffable persuasive song,
through which a mortal can charm the spirits of the
immortals.[85]

Such a passage is particularly revealing because it reveals Hekate not as sinister (as often seems to be the case for moderns) but as akin to the Christian figure of Sophia, that is, as divine guide and revealer who heeds the calls of those who are pure or purified.

Now there were ways of connecting humans with gods in temples and elsewhere. Philostratus, in his *Vita Apollonii*, remarks that in the temple of Apollo at Delphi were "golden iynges" hung in the air, which had "the persuasive power of the Sirens."[86] Iynges [plural form of iynx] were images hung in the temple by cords that were seen as "persuading" or "pulling in" the gods or a god, along the lines implied in the verses above about Hekate coming to earth because of a "persuasive song." Here the persuasion is via the image or series of images hung in the air. A single device or wheel was the iynx (from which we get our modern word "jinx") referring to a particular kind of theurgic wheel on which (in this case) iynges are mounted.

An exquisite example of an iynx is found in the Boston Museum of Fine Arts. Made of a bisque clay, the terracotta device features eleven birds with elongated necks, called "wry-necks." The bird's necks are extended and resemble the heads and necks of serpents, but also have a somewhat phallic aspect, their heads and necks like penises, their bodies like scrotums.[87] They are marked above with lines and dots, as well as below with jagged crosshatches, like lightning, as if to conduct energy. Underneath, the wheel is decorated with a series of vesica pisces that have been described as "leaves," but that do resemble the eye-like forms of engorged vulvae. There are ten "eyes" on one side, twelve on the other, hence matching the eleven birds in a sequence of ten, eleven, twelve.

The iynx was suspended from cords, and whirled in order to create a particular sound that was intended to call in the gods. The cords would bind together when it spun, and the binding was itself part of the spell or the call, symbolizing the uniting of the two (or more) into one. Iynxes were said to be effective for this reason also in love magic, and in fact there are a number of versions of them, often a wheel with four spokes, sometimes with a bird-figure spread-eagled on it, sometimes with a stylized serpent.[88] The sexual charge of the image is entirely appropriate for fertility or love magic. But the iynx also served as a theurgic device to invoke a god or gods, in particular, Hekate.

The later Platonists developed a sophisticated cosmology and metaphysics in which Hekate played an essential role not only as guide, as in the Samothracian tradition, but also as the spiritual principle of that which crosses over and allows the crossing over of boundaries. In some respects, the principle of Hekate (the cosmic soul) helps clarify the fundamental question of how the cosmos came into being out of transcendence or, to put it another way, of how that which can be quantified came into being from that which cannot be. Hekate is the principle of transmission as well as transition between realms.

Iynx-wheels and collections of iynges, or "divine seals," whether used by individual practitioners in order to invoke the gods (theurgy) or by communities in temples or telesteria, are based in the same principles represented in Pythagoreanism, that is, that all the realms of existence (the cosmos as a whole) manifest celestial harmonic principles. When one has the right harmonic forms and sounds, one can invoke or manifest the higher principle(s) in the lower realm and "extend" them horizontally. This is a shorthand definition of theurgy, that is, of conveying the gods and balancing or harmonizing the world.

The Pythagorean and the pre-Socratic tradition more broadly reflects an archaic tradition sometimes identified as "shamanic," and at this point we are really beginning to touch upon truly archaic Indo-European traditions. Such a term as "shamanic," though only an approximation, at least indicates the kind of archaic tradition represented by both Parmenides and Empedocles. But we do not have an exact terminology for these authors, whose poetic fragments also speak to our theme in this chapter. Parmenides refers to "horses" that were conveying him to the goddess herself, the wheels of his chariot fiery and calling out an ethereal sound. The goddess

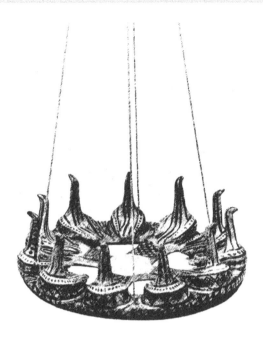

Figure 11-1. Sketch of an ancient Greek Iynx-wheel (ca. eighth century B.C.E.).

Figure 11-2. Underside of the iynx-wheel.

welcomes him, saying her maidens had accompanied him there, and says she will tell him the way of truth and distinguish it from mere human opinion.[89] Was one form of this goddess Hekate?

Here we begin to see the outlines of the primordial mysteries at the heart of Samothrace. There is a goddess, the cosmic soul envisaged in female form, and her maidens; there is a hierophant who experiences her directly; and it may be that there are twin hierophants, one who belongs to this world and another in the timeless empyrean realm, with Hekate as both the guide and the revealed goddess. The mysteries are those of communication between the divine and the human world, intimations of the paradisal islands of the blessed, Elysium, the placeless place of many names.

The island of Samothrace was sacred from time immemorial, with its sacred mountain, and hot springs, its sacred cave, and its sanctuary with temples that provided the home for the Mysteries. It was sacred long before the Romans, long before the Greeks, probably before the Pelasgians, whoever they were, and one might speculate that the kind of hierophant described by Parmenides and Empedocles—the hero, healer, and priest, the prophet and seer, the magus or theurge and poet-musician all in one—represents the most archaic figure, whom Orpheus also symbolizes. This archaic hierophant is the primordial dweller on the island, the first one, but the one who belongs to no time, indeed, is beyond time.

Samothrace is home to exactly this kind of truly archaic Greek tradition. It is not the only such home—Greece has a great many sacred places, acropoli, homes to the Mysteries, islands each with their own sacred history. And indeed, Western Europe has innumerable such sacred sites, which effectively are each an omphalos, or "navel of the earth," marking a primordial juncture of horizontal time and vertical timelessness. The pre-Socratics, the Platonic tradition, the Mysteries, all gave voice to this greater archaic unity of culture and nature. The Greek miracle as a whole was an extraordinary creative outpouring that manifested this archaic unity in perfect temple columns and architecture, in song, in poetry and myths, in philosophy and in artistry of exquisite beauty and astonishing variety.

The essential question for us, in the present era, is the extent to which these primordial mysteries are still there for us today. Many of the ancient philosophical and religious texts, including the fragments of *The Chaldean Oracles*, and of the various Pythagorean, pre-Socratic, and Platonic authors, warn against becoming subjugated to our reactions to and experiences in the material world. In our era, that which can be grasped with the hands is all that matters; ours is an era in which the sacred sites as well as the ancient teachings and myths, and the gods and goddesses of which they spoke, are all entirely ignored and forgotten. It would seem that the eclipse of the archaic world of the hierophant could not be more complete. In such a world, how could the archaic mysteries still be present?

But if the archaic sacred sites and the ancient philosophical and religious works point toward what is timeless, then it must still be accessible today, because by definition what is timeless must always be present. We traveled to Samothrace in order to make that connection, but it is not necessary to make that difficult journey to begin to connect with our indigenous, archaic European tradition, and with the intelligible realm in which the gods dwell. What is necessary, rather, is a different kind of journey, a journey of the spirit, what we may term a spiritual coming home. To this homecoming, we now turn.

Chapter 12
Coming Home

And so we come to our journey's final chapter, in which our ship leaves the harbor and the island is once again shrouded in mist behind us. The peak of Mount Saos is already cloudhidden, and we are reminded again, standing on the deck, that the island seems to generate its own unique weather. Behind us, the white wake of the ship widens, and dolphins sport near it, while ahead is the long way home. But what is home? Of course, there is our familiar homestead, a farmhouse far off in rural America. And we certainly recognize the archaic religious theme of the hearth. We are returning to ours. At the same time, there are larger themes we are engaging here as well, for our returning home is also a metaphor with multiple implications. For in some sense, perhaps we are all engaged in returning home.

By "returning home," I mean that now, for the first time in millennia, we are seeing widespread efforts to reconnect with our collective archaic past, with pagan religions and with pre-monotheistic religious traditions of Western Europe. After millennia of monotheistic opprobrium and destruction of sacred sites (to which the ruins of the Sanctuary on Samothrace bear mute witness), for the first time it is possible for Westerners to begin to re-establish ancient connections and traditions, to understand, accept, embrace, and restore their own inheritances from the past and their archaic connections to ancestral lands and sacred landscapes.

Our journey to Samothrace, and our engagement with the many facets of its esoteric mysteries, expresses our larger aim of restoring our deep links to indigenous Europe. Here I am using the word "indigenous" in what is perhaps a provocative way to allude to what I would term our European spiritual ancestry. It is no accident that the original inhabitants of Samothrace were said to have been autochthonous. What that means—sprung from the very earth—in this case is that those who recognized the island's sacredness were by connecting with it born anew by that contact. The island is where nature and culture (moving through horizontal time) intersect the vertical transcendent. Such places are unique geographically, and to be in touch with them, to understand their mythological and cultural meanings, is to begin to engage with our European and Indo-European archaic past in new and living ways.

Contemporary paganism, if it is to begin to flourish more broadly, needs to recognize its own cosmological and metaphysical inheritance and contexts. Particularly important in this process of recognition is engagement with the ancient Greek and Roman sources, not only the hints left in the mythological and historical records but also the philosophical and religious texts of late antiquity, especially those of the Platonists. There is an immense treasure in the writings of Plato, Plotinus, Iamblichus, and Damascius, to name only a few of the greatest, and those who wish to make contact with the archaic roots of Europe would be wise to explore and become deeply familiar with their works.

In the works of the Platonic tradition, and more broadly in the Greek philosophico-religious tradition, we find keys to understanding the ancient Mysteries not only in terms of the individual parts of the great puzzle of Samothrace, which we've explored in successive chapters, but also as a whole. And this larger context for understanding is provided especially by the works of the late Platonists, in particular in explanations of the Mysteries presented by Proclus, Porphyry, and Iamblichus, as well as in the fragments we have of the ancient oracles, including *The Chaldean Oracles*.

Ancient Greek religion as understood in this tradition has to do with perfecting ways in which we dwellers in this material world can provide vehicles for, unite with, and be transmuted into the divine realm. Oracles were widely known in and an important part of the ancient Greek world, but it is not always appreciated that oracles should be understood in a larger context that clarifies the meaning of many related religious practices. An oracle is a purified and consecrated individual—might be a virgin young woman, might be a child or adolescent, might be someone who has the natural or cultivated ability—who can serve as a vehicle for a god or goddess.

Just as an oracle is a consecrated individual serving as a vehicle for a god—often Apollo or Hekate—so too a statue can serve as a vehicle. Such a statue is consecrated by what is known as the telestic art, from the Greek telein–, τελεῖν, meaning to accomplish, complete, fulfill, or perfect. A consecrated statue is not just brass, wood, or marble, that is, it is not just material, but also has an invisible dimension invoked by a theurgist with liturgical and other ritual practices. Thus, for instance, a statue of Hekate might be consecrated not only with ritual invocations but also with special herbs and incenses that include rue and aromatic gums, done at the time of the waxing moon.[90]

The telestic art is sometimes termed "animating" statues, but this term is not quite right, because the telestic art means that one provides a vehicle in which gods can dwell even though they belong to an empyrean invisible realm. Hence the gods themselves say through an oracle that although they are themselves immaterial and invisible [asomatoi], bodies can become vehicles for their self-revealed nature.[91] The invisible divine realm is revealed or indicated through symbols, hence for instance Hekate's three or two heads, her three bodies, the symbols she carries like a key, two torches, a sword, and a serpent. The telestic art consists in preparing a suitable vehicle on earth for the divine to manifest itself in, perfecting [*teleste*] what is in this world that it might receive what is beyond it.

Statues are one form of telestic art, and oracles are another.[92] They are both purified vehicles, but the individual practitioner, like the statue, is adorned with the symbols and the characteristics that make the manifestation of the god possible. Those who wear specially symbolic clothing or jewelry, in a special place, with special diet, and so forth, maybe become oracles with whom one could converse. Essentially, this describes also the telestic art of the theurgist, who seeks through ritual practice and through particular symbols, sounds, scents, gestures, and ritual instruments like the iynx, to perfect himself so that it is possible to invoke a god or goddess, but also so that after death one is oneself perfected and can pass through the underworld and enter into paradise.

So too, some *places* are also conducive to the telestic art, sacred sites that are specially conducive to vehicles for the gods, places on earth where the veil is more translucent, and the gods can more easily manifest their presence. We have been to many such sacred sites throughout Western Europe, of which Samothrace is but one. Such a place is indicated by various recognizable characteristics—a high point, sacred springs, particular directional orientation, a large body of water, a mountain, a valley, a sea, an island—all of which taken together as we have seen are characteristic of Samothrace, but not only of it. Here, Samothrace is synecdochic—through it, we see the pattern of the others, each of which is also unique. Such places are not found only in Western Europe—I have visited them in North America as well, sometimes in the most surprising places, like a prehistoric grotto in the midst of a sprawling megalopolis, little changed from seven thousand years ago. But a telesterion is a sacred place specifically devoted to the telestic art, and in this respect it expresses something very rare about the ancient Greek world.

The ancient Mystery buildings were meant to intensify the telestic art, hence the name for the initiatory building, the *telesterion*, the place where initiations, human perfecting toward gods, took place. One can imagine what it must have been like to walk into an ancient telesterion from a primordial and highly symbolic landscape into a building of sacred stones, past winged angelic daimons on the ends of the building, past flaming torches, through the entryway into the *sanctum sanctorum* where along the sides are benches with carved lion-feet, above perfectly formed square patterns in the ceiling, on the far altar end two pillars, each with serpents entwined around them, spiraling to the top where the pillar becomes a carved flame. To enter such a place is to enter into the realm of the gods while on earth.

We may think that such a magnificent place belongs only to the ancient past, but our time at Samothrace has shown us that this is not quite true. There is a sense in which the cranes and chains, the ancient pieces of pillars laid out in scattered rows, indeed, the catalogues of modern archaeology, for whatever knowledge they add, are also a profanation. For although they do add to our material knowledge of the various archaeological sites, they don't acknowledge, perhaps can't acknowledge, that what once stood in such a place could stand here again, not as a dead replica but as a living exemplar of our archaic present and future. Standing on the site of the hieron, we could envision someone walking into a new telesterion of living stone, walking at once into the past and into the future present.

But the secrets of the Mysteries, while mutely embedded in the sacred stones, are alluded to in detail in the works of the Platonists. There are, of course, reasons for this. By the late third and early fourth centuries of the common era, the Mysteries, while still being celebrated collectively in some sacred sites, also had been individualized through what became known as the Pythagorean-Platonic practice of theurgy, literally, "divine working." Theurgists clearly and explicitly based their ritual work on the ancient Mysteries, but conducted their rituals individually or in small groups, often at night and outdoors in wild areas. By understanding the theurgic tradition, we see much that illuminates the Mystery traditions out of which it came and which it reflects.

In Iamblichus's *De Mysteriis* [*On the Mysteries*], he explicitly connects the practice of theurgy to the ancient Mystery traditions, particularly those that derive from Egypt, but also from what has become known as a Chaldean theurgic tradition whose central text was *The Chaldean Oracles*. Iamblichus spends considerable time noting the specific characteristics displayed by gods, archangels, angels, daemons, and heroes when they are invoked, so that they can easily be recognized. All of them are characterized by light, but of very different qualities—the gods are so overwhelming in their illumination as to make the sun, moon, and earth disappear, while each of the subsequent ranks are also illuminating, that of the heroes is characterized by fire and that of the lower orders increasing levels of darkness.[93] The gods' presence is characterized, Iamblichus tells us, by liberation from the passions, a transcendent perfection, and divine love and bliss.[94]

It is clear, from the writings or fragments of the theurgists' writings we possess, that theurgic practices followed the same course as the Mysteries. That is, the theurgist would engage in a ritual process that began with the purification of the soul, including ablution or lustration, followed by invocations based on ancient ritual language, which functioned as divine passwords or keys to allow the theurgist to cross the veils between the human and the supercelestial realms and to directly experience the divine presence. Hence in *The Chaldean Oracles* we read that the Transcendent does not receive the soul until it emerges from forgetfulness and speaks a word, remembering the pure token it had been given.[95] The ritual word is one's password as one is called to ascend into the center of the divine light.[96] We will recall that the ancient Mysteries at Samothrace and Eleusis also centered on the revelation of divine light.

But before the revelation of light, the individual would have to die to the things of this earth. Hence there would be a period of ritual death, just as in the ancient Mysteries of Samothrace and Eleusis, symbolized by the descent of Persephone and Demeter into the underworld, which symbolically is the descent of our own soul into incarnation and attachment to the material world. During this part of the ritual, one might well see phantasms, which symbolically represents the attachments and aversions drive our own reactions to the things of this world.[97] Hence this is also a period of doubledness, that is, of the individual feeling fear and separation. Plato alluded to this when he slyly said that some [the Orphics] say this body is a kind of tomb for the soul, and that philosophy is the practice of dying before one dies.[98]

And the practice of dying before one dies is exactly what the Platonic theurgists, like the celebrants of the ancient Mysteries, also said they were engaged in. That is, instead of being trapped in an afterlife as a "shade," the theurgic initiate, having directly experienced the transcendent light of "circumsplendent" divine illumination in this life, after death enters the empyrean realm or Elysium and becomes a dweller in light. Such a person, it is said, may come back to be reincarnated on earth, or become a source of illumination for later aspirants who could be conjoined with him.[99]

The theurgists describe what happens when one invokes a particular god[dess]: one sees apparitions of a flashing horse, or a boy astride a brilliantly bright horse. And the earth may grow dark, earthly light overcome by the splendor of the divine light, marked by lightning-like bolts, then giving way to a formless fire, from which comes a voice or an abundant spiraling light.[100] This probably describes the invocation of Hekate. And Hekate is the ideal goddess because, as Lewy beautifully puts it, she always encounters "human souls in forms always adequate to their internal conditions: for those sunk in the body she was necessity, for the erring, demonic temptation; for the renegade, a curse; for those who recalled their divine nature, a guide; and for those who returned home, grace."[101] "Her capacity to sympathize with all individual needs, without herself abandoning the norm of perfect existence, aroused between her and her worshippers a sympathy in which a genuine feeling of personal religion found expression."[102] Hekate includes the full gamut from chthonic "dog" daemons, the underworld, and the darkness of night to the voice from the fire, all the way to the transcendent divine light.

Hekate is often depicted bearing two torches, which would mark the sides of a doorway or entrance, a liminal space of passage. Doubleness is part of her nature, as she is at once supercelestial and chthonic, at once above and herebelow in the sublunary realm with her avenging dogs, at once belonging to the empyrean and to the earthly. Hence she was sometimes said to have two faces, like Janus, on a more esoteric level referring to both the revelation of light in creation (a face looking toward creation) and its perception (a face looking back toward the light; the initiate). Hekate represents the cosmic Mother and the cosmic matrix, the soul of the universe as a whole, as both a guide toward and an hypostasis of Rhea, only one of many names for the Great Mother through whom existence ceaselessly comes into being. One of Hekate's symbols is the spiraling snake, just like those that adorned the pillars and the seal at Samothrace. It is the spiraling symbol of the cosmic soul.[103] Hekate is said to "be visible on all sides" and to have "faces on all sides," "receiving into her womb the processions from the intelligible realm," and "send[ing] forth the channels of corporeal life."[104]

The gnostic journey of the initiate through the Mystery process, Proclus summarizes this way:

> A certain knowledge of the way of things is engendered within us by superior beings, revealed by autoptic manifestations and the guidance of the gods, who disclose the order of the universe to souls, guide our journey to the Intelligible, and kindle the fires that lead upward.[105]

This captures succinctly the Mystery tradition in which the initiate was guided to autoptically perceive the light of the god as the self-disclosure of the god in the initiate. The essential mythos: that the individual is lost in the darkness of the material world, but through the telestic art the pneumatic vehicle can be freed [through divine fire] of defilements and can be guided by the god to the realm of light and of the god.[106] That, in brief, is the work of the Mystery tradition.

Given all the texts and fragments we have, it seems pretty clear that the spiritual phenomena of light, described by the theurgists as well as alluded to in the oracular literature, refers to authentic induced experiences. That is, the theurgist invoked a god, and as a result there were corresponding phenomena, some ephemeral, some said to be more enduring. What is more, the theurgists themselves, historically of course close to if not contemporaneous with the Mystery traditions, consistently referred to their initiatory phenomena as belonging to the Mystery tradition more broadly. The theurgic tradition, like Plato's own work, directly reflects the archaic Mystery traditions, one signal representative of which was certainly on the island of Samothrace.

And there is behind all the particular goddesses, gods, and their ministers, archaic Indo-European religion that is the forebear of numerous spiritual traditions across Western Europe. The great megalithic tradition of Western Europe, with its countless dolmens and rings and rows of standing stones, bears mute but eloquent testimony to the truly archaic dimensions of European religion, hints of which are visible on Samothrace as well. To begin to understand these ancient monuments, one must go there and let them speak directly from the spiritual landscape.

But the Neoplatonists offered another way. They present us with the clues and hints necessary to recreate the Mysteries of antiquity, just as they themselves did. The last of the Platonists, recognizing the ascent to power of confessional Christianity and the looming disappearance of the archaic Mysteries, provided indications in their writings of the nature of the Mysteries dependent on no particular place or time. Theurgy is the individualization of the ancient Mysteries, conveying their keys to a future age.

We have occasionally mentioned the Chaldean oracles, which were so important for the later Platonists. The "Chaldean" religious tradition brings together ancient Greek and Roman religion with an Indo-European tradition, probably conveyed through Persia, with Egyptian and Babylonian aspects as well. The Neoplatonists drew from many sources in order to recover and to convey the nature of the Mysteries from their time to our own. And their metaphysical system, in many regards the summary achievement of antiquity, bears some very interesting connections to another tradition of that time, coming from the East—Buddhism.

That there were many deep connections between ancient Greece and Buddhism is well known, and indeed there is a term for this ancient fusion, Greco-Buddhism. It began with the extraordinary achievements of Alexander the Great, the Greek ruler and commander of the fourth century B.C.E., whose army went all the way to India and who established a Greek presence and Greco-Buddhist interconnections from that time forward. We know for certain that the Buddhist artistic tradition from Gandharan statuary onward owes its perfection to the Greek artistic tradition, but the connections between Greek and Buddhist philosophy and religious practices have not yet been fully explored.

Tibetan Buddhism carries in it gods and ritual practices whose origin is in archaic India, just as the Greek tradition carried in it gods and ritual practices from a far earlier time. Samothrace, with its ritual language no one any longer understood, is certainly an example of that. Both traditions, in short, draw from a truly archaic Indo-European well. What is more, it may be that the ancient Greek tradition has at its heart a transcendence of self and other very much akin to what we see in Buddhism, and this transcendence was in turn carried into European Christian mysticism by Dionysius the Areopagite.

In fact, it may be that the best way to understand Christianity is not as an offshoot of Judaism but as a new form of Mystery religion, with the transcendence of self and other, and with a religion of light at its heart. Is Jesus's harrowing of hell not akin to the descent into the underworld and return in the Mysteries? Seeing Christianity in this way, as a Mystery religion, would take away the longstanding conflict between confessional forms of Christianity and the ancient pagan roots of Europe, and Christianity would become another Mystery religion manifesting the religion of light very much as the Platonists saw and practiced it. That is undoubtedly the tradition inaugurated by the pseudonymous Dionysius the Areopagite, who may himself have been in actuality one of the

Neoplatonists, and it is hinted at by Schelling when he wrote about Samothrace and the ancient Greek religion.

We today live in a world of palimpsestic traditions, one atop another, and in fact it is possible that one tradition might well help shed light upon another, especially if the traditions ultimately have a common root in great antiquity. Certainly for Chandhi and me, Buddhist meditation and ritual practice has opened aspects of the ancient Greek religious tradition at Samothrace that otherwise doubtless would have remained inaccessible and opaque. And it is even possible, as John Myrdhin Reynolds has speculated, that Tibetan Buddhism and the gnostic traditions of Greek late antiquity might well share common roots. Without doubt, in any case, Buddhism has given us keys for understanding the truly archaic traditions of Europe, and this may well be because they share archaic Indo-European origins.

But beyond particular traditions, there is the truly primordial. Here we refer to the two of us as the primordial human couple on the island of the blessed. This primordiality does not require going to one sacred site, not even Samothrace, but rather speaks to us of where we are now, and who we are beyond the constraints of time and space. That is the true message from ancient Samothrace, that we are ultimately from light and of light, and that we can realize who we are—where we are right now. The journey is not outward, but inward, and the Platonists as well as the Buddhists provide maps for it, if we would like to investigate further. For what we are investigating is not a place, and not a time, but the primordial nature of reality itself.

Notes

1. See Cornelius Tacitus, *Annals*, 2.54.
2. See Diodorus Siculus, 5.48.4; see also Susan Guettel Cole, *Theoi Megaloi: The Cult of the Great Gods at Samothrace* (Leiden: Brill, 1984), 11.
3. See Varro, ap Serv. ad Virg. Aen., 8.275.
4. See Marvin Meyer, ed., *The Ancient Mysteries: A Sourcebook of Sacred Texts* (University of Pennsylvania Press, 1987), 102–3.
5. Roberto Calasso, *Literature and the Gods*, trans. Tim Parks (New York: Knopf, 2001), 5.
6. See Roberto Calasso, *The Marriage of Cadmus and Harmony*, trans. Tim Parks (New York: Knopf, 1993), 95.
7. See Nora Dimitrova, *Theoroi and Initiates in Samothrace: The Epigraphical Evidence* (Princeton: American School of Classical Studies at Athens, 2008), 84. Here one can find a translation of the epitaph of one Isidoros Nikostratou of Athens, who as "an initiate,

great-hearted," "saw the doubly sacred light of Kabiros in Samothrace," after which in death it is expected that "gloomy Hades" will himself transport Isidoros "to the Region of the Revenant and place him there."

8. See Henry Corbin, *The Man of Light in Iranian Sufism* (New Lebanon, NY: Omega, 1994), 33–34.

9. See also Apuleius's treatise "On the God of Socrates" (*De Deo Socratis*).

10. See Henry Corbin, *The Man of Light in Iranian Sufism*, 41, 56. Corbin also refers to cross-cultural comparisons that include Indo-European and even Taoist sources.

11. On the Pelasgians settling Samothrace, see Herodotus, II.51.

12. See Herodotus, II.54–57; see on the Pelasgians, I.56–58.

13. See Marvin Meyer, ed., *The Ancient Mysteries: A Sourcebook* (University of Pennsylvania Press, 1999), 106. Orphic Hymn 38, 1–25, rendition by the present author.

14. Strabo, *Geography*, Book VII.52.

15. Dimitrova, *Theoroi and Initiates in Samothrace*, 84.

16. Dimitrova, 244–45.

17. See Plutarch, *De anima*, fragment 178.

18. See Varro, *De Ling. Lat.*, 5.10.58

19. Pausanius, 9.25.6

20. See Iamblichus, *de Myst.*, 10.5–6.

21. See my discussion of this in "The Legacy of Monolatry," in Versluis, *The Mystical State* (Minneapolis: New Cultures Press, 2012), 25–32.

22. See Diodorus Siculus, 5.64.3–5.
23. See Plato, *The Republic*, 363–67.
24. See Hippolytus, *Refutation of All Heresies*, 5.8.9, cited in Walter Burkert, "Concordia Discors," in *Greek Sanctuaries: New Approaches*, ed. Nanno Marinatos and Robin Hägg, 178–91 (London: Routledge, 1993), 182.
25. See Homer, *Iliad*, 4.219; and Pindar, *Pythian Ode*, 4.
26. Aristophanes, *The Clouds*, lines 750–55.
27. Plato, *Gorgias*, 513.
28. See Arthur Versluis, *Platonic Mysticism: Contemplative Science, Philosophy, Literature, and Art* (Albany: SUNY P, 2017).
29. Plato, *Cratylus*, 407b.
30. See Livy, 45.6.3.
31. See Friedrich Wilhelm Joseph Schelling, *Treatise on the Deities of Samothrace: A Translation and an Interpretation,* trans. Robert F. Brown (Missoula, MT: Scholars Press, 1977).
32. Schelling, *On the Deities of Samothrace*, 24.
33. Schelling, *On the Deities of Samothrace*, 28–29.
34. See F. W. J. Schelling, *Philosophy and Religion*, trans. Klaus Ottmann (Putnam, CT: Spring Pub., 2010), 15.
35. Schelling, *Philosophy and Religion*, 14.
36. Schelling, *Philosophy and Religion*, 53.
37. Schelling, *Philosophy and Religion*, 54.
38. Schelling, *Philosophy and Religion*, 55.
39. He is leaving aside the various forms of Gnostic Christianity like the Valentinian, which clearly were presenting a type of Christian Mystery

religion, to focus on the kinds of Christianity that continued forward historically and were not extirpated by variants of confessional Christianity.

40. See Arthur Versluis, *Perennial Philosophy* (Minneapolis: New Cultures Press, 2015).

41. See Stobaeus, *Florilegium*, 120, 28, quoting Plutarch, *On the Soul* [attributed to Themistius].

42. Schelling, *Philosophy and Religion*, 9.

43. See Sharon Paice MacLeod, *Celtic Myth and Religion* (Jefferson, NC: McFarland, 2012), 89–99.

44. See Alexander Thom and A. S. Thom, *Megalithic Remains in Britain and Brittany* (Oxford: Oxford University Press, 1978), 100.

45. See John Michell, "Megalithic Science: An Essay on the Origins and Uses of Old Stone Monuments," in *The Old Stones of Land's End* (London: Garnstone, 1974), 107–33.

46. Tacitus, *Annals,* 2.54.2–4.

47. See Plutarch, *Apothegmata Lakonika.*

48. Clement of Alexandria, *Exhortation to the Heathens,* 2.15.

49. See Diodorus Siculus, 4.4.1.

50. See Nonnus, *Dionysiaca,* 48.962. "The Athenians honored Iakkhos the third Dionysus, as a god next after the son of Persephoneia [Zagreus the first Dionysus], and after Semele's son [Dionysus the second]. They . . . chanted a new hymn for Iakkhos (Iacchus). In these three celebrations [of the three incarnations of Dionysus] Athenians reveled."

51. See Euripides, *The Bacchae;* Diodorus Siculus, 5.48.2.

52. See Daniel Ogden, *Drakon: Dragon Myth and Serpent Cult in the Greek and Roman Worlds* (New York: Oxford University Press, 2013), 215–46. See also for an exceptional collection of classical sources on dragons and serpents in Greco-Roman antiquity, Daniel Ogden, *Dragons, Serpents, and Slayers in the Classical and Early Christian Worlds* (New York: Oxford University Press, 2013).

53. See [Pseudo] Aristotle, *Mirabilium auscultationes*, 845b.

54. See Valerius Flaccus, *Argonautica*, 8.54–121, cited in Ogden, *Dragons, Serpents, and Slayers*, 129, 147–48.

55. Ogden, *Drakon*, 273.

56. Ogden, *Drakon*, 276–77.

57. Julian, *Orations*, 6.17; Lucian, *Demonax*, 63.

58. See Claude Lecouteux, *Demons and Spirits of the Land* (Rochester, VT: Inner Traditions, 2015), 158–61.

59. See Homer, *Iliad,* 23.277; see also Lucan, *Pharsalia*, 6.396.

60. See Virgil, *Georgics*, iv.387–395, where Proteus is associated with Thrace, Thessaly, and prophetic powers; see also Valerius Flaccus, *Argonautica*, 2.318.

61. See Strabo, *Geography*, 10.3.21.

62. Homer, *Odyssey*, 4.365.

63. See also Hesiod, *Theogony*, 240 ff.

64. See Pausanius, *Description of Greece*, 2.22.1.

65. Ovid, *Metamorphoses*, 4.605.

66. Pausanius, *Description of Greece*, 2.37.6.

67. Lucan, *Pharsalia*, 3.399–413.

68. See Lecouteux, *Demons and Spirits of the Land*, 30–31, citing the *Homilia de sacrilegiis* (eighth century), the seventh-century Synod of Nantes, and so forth.

69. See Walter Burkert, *Greek Religion,* trans. John Raffan (Cambridge: Harvard University Press, 1985), 285, citing Felix Jacoby, *Die Fragmente der grieschischen Historiker* (Berlin, 1923–58), 823 F1.

70. See Walter Burkert, *Greek Religion*, 285, 459.

71. Strabo, *Geography*, 10.3.19–21. It is noteworthy that Melinoe was an Orphic name for Hekate; the name may be another connection between the island of Samothrace (with its cave of Hekate) and the goddess Hekate in her various manifestations. See *Orphic Hymn*, 71.

72. Strabo, *Geography*, 10.3.7–9.

73. Strabo, *Geography*, 10.3.7–9.

74. One of the names claimed by some of the Church Fathers for the primordial man of the Samothracian Mysteries was "Adamna." See for instance Hippolytus, *Refutation*, 5.8.9, as well as the discussion of Burkert in *Greek Religion*, 458–59, note 49. Is it that the name is truly archaic and genuinely was in use at Samothrace, or is it that the name is comparable to the meaning of primordial man?

75. Walter Burkert, *Greek Religion*, 134–35.

76. See Diodorus Siculus, *Library of History*, 5.48.2.

77. See Empedocles, *Purifications*, B112-B147.

78. A term coined by Ernest Renan, "Prayer on the Acropolis," in *Souvenirs d'enfance et de jeunesse* (Paris: 1883/1897).

79. A gloss on the phrase "dogs are slain"—in *The Chaldean Oracles*, and in the Platonic tradition, the "dogs" are the avenging daemons that punish mortal sins, and in this context, "slaying dogs" could be understood esoterically as Hekate providing a "pass" from one realm to the next, past one's avenging "dogs." See *Chaldean Oracles*, fragment 90, referring to "chthonian dogs" [daemons] that seek to keep one trapped in the material realm.

80. Lycophron, *Alexandra*, 74 ff., 1174 ff.

81. Strabo, *Geography*, 10.3.20, 10.3.10.

82. Nonnus, *Dionyiaca*, 13.400; see also 4.184.

83. See for instance, Hesiod, *Theogony*, 404 ff.

84. Orpheus, *Argonautica*, 975.

85. See *The Chaldean Oracles*, fragment 219, version by the author. See for the full text Ruth Majercik, trans., *The Chaldean Oracles* (Dilton Marsh, UK: Prometheus, 2015).

86. See Philostratus, *Vita Apollonii* [*Life of Apollonius of Tyana*], 6.11.

87. See Grace W. Nelson, "A Greek Votive Iynx-wheel in Boston," *American Journal of Archaeology* 44, no. 4 (Dec. 1940): 443–56. See especially 447–48, where she remarks on the association with "love magic" and "fertility magnet," as well as the serpentine and fascinating phallic look of the birds themselves.

88. See Sarah Johnston, *Hekate Soteira: A Study of Hekate's Roles in the Chaldean Oracles and*

Related Literature (Atlanta: Scholars Press, 1990), 98 ff.

89. See, for a lively translation of the poetic fragments of Parmenides and Empedocles, Stanley Lombardo, trans., *Parmenides and Empedocles* (San Francisco: Grey Fox, 1982), for instance, 11–13.

90. See *The Chaldean Oracles*, fragment 224.

91. Proclus, *In Rempublicam*, II.242.812

92. See Iamblichus, *De mysteriis*, 5.23

93. See Iamblichus, *De mysteriis*, 2.4

94. Iamblichus, *De mysteriis*, 2.9.

95. See *The Chaldean Oracles*, 109; see also 2.

96. See *The Chaldean Oracles*, 110–11.

97. See Proclus, *Commentary on Alcibiades*, 340.1, wherein he remarks that during the Eleusinian Mysteries terrifying phantoms became visible to the initiates. See Hans Lewy, *Chaldean Oracles and Theurgy: Mysticism, Magic, and Platonism in the Later Roman Empire* (Paris: Études Augustiniennes, 1978), 238.

98. See Plato, *Cratylus*, 400b. "For some say the body is the tomb of the soul—I think it was the followers of Orpheus in particular who introduced this word." See also *Phaedo*, 62b, 82d-e; and *Gorgias*, 493a.

99. See Hans Lewy, *Chaldean Oracles and Theurgy*, 224–25.

100. See *Chaldean Oracles*, fragments 146 and 148. See also Proclus, *Commentary on the Republic*, 1.111.1; and Lewy, *Chaldean Oracles and Theurgy*, 240–41.

101. Lewy, *Chaldean Oracles and Theurgy*, 365.

102.   Lewy, *Chaldean Oracles and Theurgy*, 365.
103.   See Plato, *Timaeus*, 36e.
104.   *Chaldean Oracles,* fragment 189, from Proclus, *In Tim.*, 2.130.23–28.
105.   *Chaldean Oracles,* fragment 190, from Proclus, *In Alc.*, 87.
106.   *Chaldean Oracles*, fragment 196.

CPSIA information can be obtained
at www.ICGtesting.com
Printed in the USA
LVHW091349060519
616783LV00001B/29/P